BOOKS BY H. ALLEN SMITH

MR. KLEIN'S KAMPF
LOW MAN ON A TOTEM POLE
LIFE IN A PUTTY KNIFE FACTORY
LOST IN THE HORSE LATITUDES
RHUBARB
LO, THE FORMER EGYPTIAN!
LARKS IN THE POPCORN
WE WENT THATAWAY
PEOPLE NAMED SMITH
MISTER ZIP
SMITH'S LONDON JOURNAL
THE COMPLEAT PRACTICAL JOKER
THE REBEL YELL
THE AGE OF THE TAIL
WRITE ME A POEM, BABY

Selected by H. Allen Smith

DESERT ISLAND DECAMERON

With Ira L. Smith

LOW AND INSIDE
THREE MEN ON THIRD

WRITE ME A POEM, BABY

Write Me a Poem, Baby

H. ALLEN SMITH

DRAWINGS BY JOHN V. MORRIS

BOSTON · Little, Brown and Company · TORONTO

The items from *The New Yorker* on pages 12, 38, 39, 43,
75, 85, 133, copyright, 1945, 1946, 1947, 1948, 1954, 1955,
The New Yorker Magazine, Inc.

Published simultaneously in Canada
by Little, Brown & Company (Canada) Limited

PRINTED IN THE UNITED STATES OF AMERICA

Children and fooles cannot lye.

JOHN HEYWOOD, *Proverbs*

AUTHOR'S NOTE

Some of the material in this book appeared originally in *Good Housekeeping* and the book itself was made possible largely through the enthusiasm of that magazine's editor, Herbert R. Mayes. I should like to thank Mr. Mayes as well as his many readers who showered me with further examples of children's writings.

H. ALLEN SMITH

Old Roaring Brook Road
Mount Kisco, New York

WRITE ME A POEM, BABY

O NCE UPON A TIME, in the olden day, about six months ago, a friend of mine told me that his two daughters, aged nine and eleven, were hard at work writing a play. They hadn't got very far with it as yet, but their father suggested that I, as a professional writer, might like to have a look at their work in progress. I agreed and he showed me the following script:

ACT I

HELENA, coming on the stage in the middle.

HELENA: I wonder what is keeping Charles Arnold, the TV repair man.

There is a knock.

HELENA: Come in. Charles Arnold comes in.

CHARLES: Where is the TV set.

HELENA: (*to Herself*) My he is very handsome considering he is only a TV repair man.

CHARLES: I am here to repair the TV set.

HELENA: It is badly broke and will be hard work so would you like to have a hi-ball.

CHARLES: No but I will take a cup of tea.
HELENA: Humf.

That was as far as the girls had gone, but it was enough to warrant certain critical observations. I said that I thought it was a splendid beginning, that among other attributes it had almost unbearable suspense. I gave it as my opinion that if the girls could maintain the pace, they'd probably have a hit show on their hands.

If I seem to have been too enthusiastic, I'd better explain that I have long been a pushover for the literary strivings of small children. They are, as a general rule, much better writers than grownups. They bring a freshness and a verve to their work that is often lacking in adult writers. Their integrity is absolute. And unconsciously they are funnier than the best of our professional humorists.

At the time I was exposed to the dramatic impact of Helena's first meeting with Charles Arnold, the TV repair man, I began recalling other examples of graphic composition by small children. Exploring my personal files, which go under the name of Snafu, I found that I had preserved a dozen or so juvenile literary works that bordered on genius. I decided I would try to find enough additional mate-

[4]

rial to make a small book. This, then, is the result. It probably has no bearing on the great controversy which has been raging in educational circles during the last year — the question of whether or not Johnny can read. There is an old story about an overgrown country bumpkin who handed his paw a sheet of paper covered with scribblings.

"Look what I wrote," said the boy.

His paw examined the paper.

"What does it say?" he asked.

"Don't know," said the son, "I ain't learned to read yet."

In the course of gathering little gems for this collection I've found out more about children than I've ever been able to learn from the prose of Spock and Gesell. Juvenilia came at me from every section of the country and in the end the over-all harvest of scribblings and scrawlings resembled an avalanche in black and white. The calligraphy in these minor manuscripts may be cockeyed and smudged, the syntax may look as if it had been struck by lightning, and the punctuation may give offense to the purists among the pedagogues, yet there is one element that sparkles and effervesces in the poems, the compositions, the stories and the letters: that element is truth.

Let us have a quick look at a magnificent piece of poetry sent to me by Mrs. Thomas B. Cracroft of Asheville, North Carolina. It was written by one of Mrs. Cracroft's fifth-graders and reads:

AUTUMN

The autumn days are here
You always expect them this time of year.

I doubt very much if Robert Frost could have said it better. And if I were a poet, no matter how great and famous, I'd hereby resolve never to tackle autumn again, never to write a line about the fall season of the year, as long as I lived. That Tarheel child has said all that can be said about it in those two lines.

Another major element to be found in the literary strivings of small children is that of surprise — the unexpected conclusion. We see it even in the above-quoted "Autumn" and we'll see it again and again as we go along. We can often anticipate the thought sequence of an adult, but it's more difficult with children. I remember the story of an incident that took place in a Long Island schoolroom back in 1943. A first-grade teacher was having difficulty teaching one little boy to read numbers. At last, in desperation, she asked the child's father to come to the school. She wanted to demonstrate to him that his son suffered under a sort of invincible ignorance when it came to identifying numbers. The father, of course, refused to believe such a libel. He walked up to the blackboard, took a piece of chalk, and wrote a large 3.

"What's that?" he said to his boy.

"Three."

He erased the 3 and wrote a big 5.

"What's that?" he asked.

"Five."

He smirked in the direction of the teacher, erased the 5 and made an 8.

"What's that?" he demanded.

"Pretzel," said his son.

That's a "bright saying" and this is not a book of "bright sayings." Our concern is with the written word and with the minor philosophers who put it on paper. Whether they're in school or at home children write on almost every conceivable subject. Nothing daunts them; no topic is too broad or too deep for them. It takes a courageous man to prescribe a cure for the national malady — worry and nervousness — for he knows he's apt to fall on his face. A child tackles the subject fearlessly. I am in possession of an essay composed by a ten-year-old philosopher in an Oregon school, a boy whose title decorations (done in red, green and blue)

suggest that he may be under the influence of H*Y*M*A*N K*A*P*L*A*N. The essay follows:

* — * DONT WORRY * — *

Dont worry There is no sense to it. Why do worms worry. Because the birds eat them. Why do birds worry. Because people shoot them and eat them. Why do calfs worry. Because people milk the milk and they dont get any. They even do it with electrisity and machines. Why do people worry. That is what I ask.

I don't contend that this boy has done any more with the problem than, say, Dr. Norman Vincent

Peale. I suspect, however, that somewhere within those few lines there may be a solid nugget — a cure for the national neurosis. It cured mine, at least for a little while.

A New England teacher tells me of a harrowing experience she underwent during a period when she was presiding over a class of seventh-graders. The children were writing compositions on subjects of their own choosing. Their little essays were to be posted around the blackboard on a day when all the parents were coming to visit the school. One boy, named Claude, got a late start and was having trouble finding a subject. Finally the teacher told him to write on "I Love Spring." All the other essays were in and the hour was approaching for the visit of the parents (who would, of course, inspect the exhibits). At last Claude handed in his paper, which went:

I LOVE SPRING

I love spring. I really do. I love spring because when spring comes my parents start having their cocktail parties outside on the terrase instead of inside. All the people come and I climb up in the tree and hide and watch them drink their cocktails. Then they all go and my parents go out to bade them good by. Then I come down and quick drink what is left in the glasses. Then

I climb back up the tree and sit there looking around. It makes me feel so good. I love spring.

What could that poor distraught teacher do? Claude's work had to be on the blackboard before

the parents arrived and she knew that he wouldn't be able to compose another essay in the time that remained. So she retired to her desk and, imitating Claude's scrawl, produced a brief but acceptable composition for him — she simply had him get up in that tree and look around and feel good and love spring without cocktails.

Years ago George Jean Nathan told me that his old friend the late Henry L. Mencken was "the only person I've ever known who had a completely and thoroughly happy childhood." Mr. Nathan's suggestion that almost all children are burdened with woe runs contrary, of course, to the traditional belief that the springtide of life is the happy time.

The enormous tensions and antagonisms of children are often reflected in their writings. A child writing a note or a letter to his parents or to other grownups usually tries to represent himself as a paragon of virtue and propriety. When he's writing in school he knows that his words are to be scrutinized by Tyrant Teacher, so he is inclined to hide the fact that he's an anarchist at heart. But when the kids address *each other* on paper, or psychoanalyze each other in their written documents, they are capable of bludgeon blows fully as powerful as any ever dealt by either Mencken or Nathan. This is especially true in the never-ending War of the Siblings. I have examined dozens of poems and compositions in which brothers go after sisters, sisters after brothers, brothers after brothers, and sisters after sisters, all armed with meat axes. One of the most straightforward of these assaults was written in a Westchester primary school by a ten-year-old boy. The pupils had been told to write poems for Thanksgiving and this boy's job of work, which was later reprinted in the *New Yorker,* read as follows:

THOUGHTS ON THANKSGIVING DAY

I have a bratty sister.
If she got lost I never would have missed her.
On the rim of the Grand Canyon, I hope,
She will slip on a piece of soap.
Though I be near
Her calls I will not hear.
Then I'd hear and turn around
And see her hurtling toward the ground.
I'm too late
To save her from her fate.
There are many who feel like this,
Whose brothers and sisters they would never miss.
Enjoy your turkey.
Happy Thanksgiving!

If you are now finished with your speculations on how that piece of soap got onto the rim of the Grand Canyon, we shall proceed to another example of child's inhumanity to child. Just recently I got my hands on a notice, done in rude block letters, which was circulated one summer in a camp for small girls in New Hampshire. It follows:

1. Kate can't sleep in our tent or come over.
2. Talk Nasty if IT shows up.
3. Kate is supposenly a little girl but act like an un-echecated animal because she is. Shes a little stinker always butting into other peoples bussiness. You can always tell when she is coming down the street. You can smell her a mile away.
4. I feel sorry for her poor sister Daphny.
5. She looks like a ape & her manners are like an ape.
6. She is sexy dirty and a slob.

The foregoing document was shown to me by the mother of the girl who wrote it. "It was sent to me," the mother explained, "by one of the camp counselors. I was shocked by the meanness in it and I was ashamed of my girl. So I made an investigation and found out that everything turned out all right. The little girl Kate walked up to my daughter in front of the whole camp one morning, slapped her in the face and then pulled her hair. Within a couple of days they had become friendly once again."

The mother said "everything turned out all right." Not for me. I'm still a little nervous about the whole situation. I'm sure that we grownups are under a heavy obligation to Mother Nature. We should be eternally grateful to her for making children so little when they are young; if they had size on their side, I suspect they might turn on us and beat our brains out with the butt ends of cap pistols.

Hilda Cole Espy has been writing for the magazines since she was in her late teens. Her output is somewhat limited today, but the literary output of her family is staggering — there are five Espy children. Four of them have been writing from the time they could grasp pencil or crayon. The fifth, little Jeff, will start his writing career very soon. He is already inventing stories about his adventures with a make-believe pal, a lad by the name of Bill Rotten.

Mrs. Espy has saved every scrap of family writing she's been able to get her hands on. Some of it will appear in later pages and a good portion of it will reflect the family's interest in animals.

The eldest daughter, Mona, composed the following when she was eleven years old:

ARE ANIMALS

Shorty. Shorty is a black dog with a white chest. He just loves attention. He also loves to go on walks. Shorty is fed once a day. He is out practically all day and in all night. His breed is Doxcent and Begle.

How dogs should be taken care of. A dog should be

fed at least once a day. Once in a while he should be given a egg. Bread and potatoes are not good for dogs. A dog should be given a lot of exercise. Do not leave dogs out at night unless they have a dog house. Never scream at a dog.

Sick animals and what to do. Ducks. Dr. Craine says

When the ducks are sick from being in the cold are their heads are hanging down give them a teaspoon full of wiskey.

I would like to make a few observations on the above essay. In the first place, some adult readers who have been in the cold are their heads are hanging down may think that what'll cure a duck will also cure a human. Having reached that conclusion, they'll look at a duck and then look at themselves and say, "Well, if a duck takes a teaspoon, then I ought to need at least a pint." They had best beware. If they insist upon taking the duck treatment,

I've figured it out for them. Most of the ducks I know weigh around five pounds. Three teaspoons make one tablespoon. Two tablespoons make one liquid ounce. In other words, it would take six sick ducks to dispose of one ounce of wiskey. A man who weighs one hundred and fifty pounds is the equivalent of thirty ducks. Therefore he is entitled to take five full ounces of wiskey *provided he has been out in the cold and his head is hanging down.*

One other observation: in her biography of Shorty, Mona overlooked his most salient characteristic. I happen to know this Shorty and it's true — his breed is Doxcent and Begle. This mixture has produced one of the most frustrated creatures on the face of the earth. A Doxcent is a home-loving dog; a Begle is a roamer, forever on the go. So there is warfare going on in the breast of Shorty all the time. He walks out of the Espy house and the Begle in him gets him as far as the public sidewalk. Then he stands there, the Begle part of him gazing off toward Adventureland. The Begle part will lead him to take a tentative step in the direction of the wide-open spaces, but instantly the Doxcent in him summons him back, and he retreats. He will sometimes spend half an hour on that sidewalk, moving

[16]

forward, then stepping back, then moving forward again, then stepping back. The neighbors think he is a dog that has been taught to fox-trot.

Since I started collecting the literature of goslings I have been associating with so many school-

teachers that, even in the seclusion of my study, I raise my hand whenever I want to leave the room. One of these teachers has preserved a sheet of paper which she confiscated one day in her sixth-grade classroom. Two little girls had been writing notes to each other, using the same sheet of paper and passing it back and forth. The readability of their dialogue was enhanced by the fact that one girl wrote with a pen while the other responded with a pencil. The entire correspondence follows:

Did you see Mr. Minten in the hall?
  I'll say. Red and white checker shirt. Yum Yum. I could go for him.
You better be carful he's got a wife.
  I know that stupid but I don't think she appresiates him.
Lets go to Windys after. He goes there sometimes for a coke.
  Swell. Joy!!!
I bet you got a 100 on your math test just because of me.
  What do you mean "because of me."
Well I gave you most of the ansers.
  Poo. I knew them already. Who do you think you are Inestein?
Don't you dare try to get nasty with me.
  You are getting to be a concieted stuck up slob.
If I thought you meant that I'd tell Miss G—— you cheated.
  I've quit talking to you you nidwit.
YOU STUCK UP CONCEITED SNOBISH BUM, BRAT, RAT.
  TAKES ONE TO CALL ONE.
Always knew you were a phony stinker.
  G O O D B Y E

Susie Clemens was thirteen at the time her father was writing *Huckleberry Finn*, a period in which she was engaged on a secret project: her own biography of Mark Twain. Susie was convinced that other people (meaning adults) who had written about her father had failed to get his essential qualities on paper and it was her aim to rectify the situation. The flavor of her own delightful study is reflected in a single sentence, which I quote:

He has the mind of an author exactly, some of the simplest things he can't understand.

Her punctuation may be slightly askew, but no sensible person would object to that. Mark Twain himself said that if there's one thing on earth a man's entitled to, it's his own punctuation. As an author I would like to say this: among all the telling sentences that came from the pen of her illustrious father, none excels Susie's for sheer perceptivity and depth. Her implication is clear — Susie understands some of the simplest things, but Papa doesn't. This in spite of the fact that Mark Twain understood more things better than almost any other adult in the history of the United States.

The muse Euterpe, who smiles on both W. H. Auden and Nick Kenney, manages to spend a lot of time visiting our elementary schools. Lyric poets are coming along in fairly large numbers in the primary grades and their work has been flowing to my desk in a slow but steady trickle. Here, for example, is a poem from the pen (or crayon) of seven-year-old Henry Lockwood of Westchester:

A FRIEND

The horse is my friend
Until the end.

And from Michael Binder, a more elderly poet of eleven:

SPRING POEM

Spring is here, and
Bringing good cheer.
Robins chirp,
Frogs burp.

Among the most celebrated one-act plays ever written in this country is that stark and soul-stirring drama *Grandmother Has Gone To The Bar — Huk*. It was written by nine-year-old Sally Wilson of Washington, D. C., and it has become famous largely through the writings of Westbrook Pegler. Sally's father is Lyle C. Wilson, vice-president of the United Press and boss of the UP Washington bureau. Mr. Pegler is an old friend of the Wilsons' and a frequent visitor in their home. When he stumbled on the manuscript of Sally's play, he recognized its true value. The complete text follows:

GRANDMOTHER HAS GONE TO THE BAR — HUK

STEP-MOTHER — I'm tired of living here, I've always wanted to be an actress.

FATHER — You certainly don't care for the children think of what they'll go threw grandmother is alwas getting drunk.

MOTHER — If the children can't get along by there self its to bad I can't help it if grandmother gets drunk.

(*Children Enter*)

JO — Guess what I don't have any homework.

FATHER — Good do you have any Clover.

CLOVER — A little bit.

DICK — A little bit my foot.

(*Grandmother Enters*)

GRANDMOTHER — I've huk squesed the potatoes, huk and pealed the huk, lemons.

MOTHER — Oh dear.

(*Children laugh and mother leaves the room*)

FATHER — Granny wouldn't you like to get some water.

GRANDMOTHER — Later on I'm going to the bar now.

JO — If you don't go to the bar more than twise a day I'll eat my hat.

GRANDMOTHER — You don't have any to eat huk.

MOTHER — Come on in and eat children.

FATHER — Grandmothers gone to the bar.

MOTHER — Thank gonnese.

FATHER — You know the children can't stay with her.

MOTHER — They are not my children where is there real mother.

FATHER — Its a long story but you remember that big tank full of gas that started leaking in Gayton well we lived a block away and I was reading a paper and my wife was soing on some close and I opened the door and a man said the gas tank was busted so I ran for the boys and my wife ran for Clover. It was so fogie outside I couldn't see.

MOTHER — The children must have had very bad mem-
    erys not to remember this.
FATHER — Well Dick was only two but he slept threw
    the whole thing Jo was one and Clover was 3
    months well the streets were crowded my wife
    sliped on a rock I don't know exactly how we got
    apart but I notised she was missing many a times
    I looked for her but i never found her.
MOTHER — How queer.

That is the end of it. I understand that Mr. Pegler, after reading it for the first time, called Sally in
and bought the world rights to the play for the sum
of one nickel. I have not asked Mr. Pegler's permission to reprint it here, but I don't expect him to file
suit; I suspect he is a little tired of courtrooms.

It must be noted, however, that there has been
more argument and discussion over Sally's play than
over any single work of James Joyce. Most of the
controversy has centered on the single word *huk*.
One school of thought, the classicists, have insisted
that the word should be *hic*. Others have argued
just as forcefully that beauty is truth, truth is beauty,
and *huk* is better than *hic*.

A second question that has been debated in every quarter of the land: is the play complete? Did
Sally intend that "How queer" should be the final
curtain line? The critics disagree and I understand

that there have been fist fights over the matter. I refuse to be dragged into the controversy and so does Sally.

Sally, in fact, is too busy. She is now Mrs. Charles B. Crawford and the mother of three potential playwrights.

If Sally Wilson had written her play in school, and the teacher had decided it was good enough for publication in the school paper (which is highly improbable), the teacher would have corrected both the spelling and the punctuation and the word *huk* would have become lost for all time. I understand *why* the teachers make such corrections, but in a way it's unfortunate. Quite often the spelling of small children is pure inspiration, as in the case of the girl who wrote:

If you do not wash your hair you will get dandrith.

Or the girl who wrote from summer camp:

I am having fun but I am angshus to come home.

Children spend a lot of time writing about the various national holidays that come along during the school year. Abraham Lincoln, for example, always gets a good press in late February. It was a Wisconsin child who supposedly wrote:

Abraham Lincoln was born in a log cabin which he built with his own hands.

My own favorite Lincoln composition was contributed by Mrs. W. D. Van Petten, who once taught school in a small Arizona town. Her fourth-grade class was made up of Mexican children. They had been studying Lincoln, so Mrs. Van Petten asked them to write something about him. One boy turned in the following paper:

After the war was over Lincoln was very tired. So he said, I think I'll go to the show. So he went to the show and was sitting on a box and a man shot him.

The father who is mentioned in the following communiqué has issued a firmly worded warning that no names are to be used. He is a large and powerful brute, so I have substituted fake names.

When the father and mother go out for the evening, their twelve-year-old daughter serves as baby sitter for two-year-old Glen. It is the daughter's custom, before she goes to bed, to write out a report to her parents. One such report follows:

Dear Mommy and Daddy,

The dishes are all done and the kitchen is fairly clean I hope! Butch and the cats have been fed. The fishes water seems to be about the right temperature. Glennie went to bed about 9:15. He's been so cute! Tonight when he said he wanted to go on the wee wee duck we were up stairs so I put him on the toilet in the upstairs bathroom. He let out a scream and in his loudest voice said, "I want to do it like daddy! Standin up and backerwards!" Then he took his bath and went to bed.

Loads of love,
Linda

That thing has given me pause. Somehow I was always under the impression that *I* was the one who was fronterwards.

Faith Baldwin, who has published upwards of eighty novels, informs me that she wrote a poem when she was ten, and its publication in a religious magazine so upset her father that she's convinced it shortened his life. It went:

> When I was young this was my cry
> Oh God why must I ever die?
> But now I'm old and sore oprest
> My cry is Lord Oh give me rest!

Even more inflammatory was the romantic couplet which Mildred Spurrier Topp says she and her sister composed when they were small children. The story is from her book, *Smile Please*. Her mother was a widow and a local judge had shown some interest and the two little girls, who favored the judge, wanted to promote his cause. Valentine's Day was approaching, so the girls decided to compose a valentine, forge their mother's name to it, and send it to the judge. Mildred felt that the fake valentine should have a suggestion of dignity and erudition behind it. She remembered a big word she had encountered in her Bible reading, a word used in connection with King Solomon, a word she felt sounded "romancy." So the valentine that was sent off to the judge read:

> If you will be my valentine,
> I will be your concubine.

Jack Kahn was born in New York City. There is some evidence that he was the boy who grew up to be Mickey Spillane. On the other hand it seems more likely that he became E. J. Kahn, Jr., one of the top writers on the *New Yorker*. The Spillane hypothesis is based solely on a single short letter written when the boy was nine. It was addressed to a schoolmate named Peter. Peter was at home ill and the fifth-grade teacher assigned young Jack Kahn to write to him and tell him what was going on at school during his absence. The letter follows:

April 9, 1926.

Dear Pete,

How are you feelin'? Are you coming back Monday? I hope so. We need you to help fight against the S. S. S. They're getting fresher every day, and Tom Taylor is getting freshest. You oughta ha' seen what he did to Pfiffer the other day. One of the S. S. S.es gave Pfiffer a black eye yesterday, and in a fight Junie just gave up because the S. S. S. guy had an unfair grip and Junie couldn't breathe. The gip is they have lots more guys, because all three sixt grades fight; Jim Malard gave Harry a nice licking, boy we were glad! You see, Malard used to be on the sixth grade's side. Four guys at once jumped on top of Scott. Imagine, four guys at once, and each one bigger than Scott was, When Junie was having a fight, he wouldn't give up, so the S. S. S.es had to haul there own guy off. Edgar gave Delacorte a dirty sock, too, and "Four-eyes" Kingleys did some dirty work. Tom Taylor with a whole bunch of sixth graders around him would come charging up and sock down everything in his way. We stood against the wall and would jump out on them as they came.

Love,
Jack K.

A single explanatory note is needed. The S. S. S. stands for Sneaky, Stinking Sixth. And one punctuational note: the Kahn letter represents one of the few times in the history of the written word that a

person under twenty years of age used a semicolon without being told to do it.

Seventy years ago Mark Twain found fascination in a manuscript which may have been the first collection of "boners" ever undertaken. A schoolteacher made the collection and titled her book *English as She is Taught*. Mark Twain used it as the basis for an essay-sermon attacking the American system of education. At the same time he reveled in the unconscious humor which he found in the little book. He reprinted one composition which he described as being "full of naivete, brutal truth, and unembarrassed directness, and is the funniest (genuine) boy's composition I think I have ever seen." Here it is:

ON GIRLS

Girls are very stuck up and dignefied in their maner and be have your. They think more of dress than anything and like to play with dowls and rags. They cry if they see a cow in a far distance and are afraid of guns. They stay at home all the time and go to church on Sunday. They are al-ways sick. They are al-ways funy and making fun of boy's hands and they say how dirty. They cant play marbels. I pity them poor things. They make fun of boys and then turn round and love them. I dont beleave they ever kiled a cat or anything. They look out every nite and say oh ant the moon lovely. Thir is one thing I have not told and that is they always now their lessons bettern boys.

Another bit from the manuscript that is much more substantial than a common boner comes under the heading of poetry analysis. The following stanza from *The Lady of the Lake* was given to a pupil:

Alone, but with unbated zeal,
The horseman plied with scourge and steel;
For jaded now and spent with toil,

Embossed with foam and dark with soil,
While every gasp with sobs he drew,
The laboring stag strained full in view.

The pupil's analysis of that passage:

The man who rode on the horse performed the whip
and an instrument made of steel alone with strong ar-
dor not diminishing, for, being tired from the time
passed with hard labor overworked with anger and ignorant with weariness, while every breath for labor he
drew with cries full of sorrow, the young deer made
imperfect who worked hard filtered in sight.

I am unable to resist including Mark Twain's
personal reaction to that splendid analysis. He
wrote:

I see, now, that I never understood that poem before. I have had glimpses of its meaning, in moments
when I was not as ignorant with weariness as usual,
but this is the first time the whole spacious idea of it
ever filtered in sight. If I were a public-school pupil I
would put those other studies aside and stick to analysis; for, after all, it is the thing to spread your mind.

The following poem was written by Ruth M.
Neirenberg of Cincinnati at the age of eight:

THE STORM

Snow, snow. White, white white
I can see it with my bad eyesight.

There was not a thing wrong with Ruth's eyesight — that was the only word she could think of to
rhyme with "white."

Out of my own attic I have resurrected a post-
card sent by my son at the age of twelve to his sister
when she was spending her first summer in camp.
His tender message:

We are sending you some cookys. They are good,
they have to be good because I helped make them. If
one of your buck teeth cracks don't worry youre only
biting a wallnut shell. Listen you moth eaten old
nanny goat don't go around that whacky camp making
any statements about my love affares or I'll kill you.

Sentiment, sweet affection, nobility and compas-
sion do sometimes appear in the correspondence of
child with child, but more often these qualities
turn up in formal composition — in rhetorical exer-
cises whether at home or in school. I'm reminded
of an episode in the office of a small-town newspaper where I worked thirty-odd years ago. One of

the owners of the paper had a twelve-year-old son who yearned to become a reporter. He usually hung around the office on Saturdays and the rest of us were required to tolerate him and be kind to him. He was forever begging for something to do. One Saturday afternoon a big story broke — three workmen were killed in a sewer construction blast. There was great excitement in the newspaper office — much intemperate yelling and racing about. The boy tried to stay out of the way, but he wanted desperately to be in on the big story. He retired to a desk at the rear of the room and began slowly pecking away at a typewriter. After perhaps an hour he came forward and placed a sheet of paper on the city editor's desk. *He* had written the big story, in its entirety, as follows:

Three men were killed in a dynamite explosion today in the new sewer. An explosion is about the worst thing than can happen to a man.

My own first *professional* writing was done on that same newspaper when, to be truthful, I was little more than a child myself. One evening I sat down before a side-winding Oliver typewriter and in less than half an hour composed the following news item:

Ed Ramsey of Bippus was visiting freinds in Huntington yesterday also buying some new horness.

I think there should have been a comma in it somewhere, to make it really perfect, but I was cool toward the comma in those days. I remember that I stayed around till three in the morning, waiting for the paper to come off the press, so I could see my first article in print. It had been wretchedly butchered and distorted. Somebody had misspelled "freinds" and then put a period after the word "yesterday," killing the final third of the article, leaving out the important information that Ed Ramsey had bought some new horness. In spite of all this editorial slaughter, however, I was proud of it. Along about daylight I went home and put a knotted silk stocking over my head, for I was training my pompadour at the time, and finally fell asleep to dream of my new-found life's profession — the writing trade.

Here is a piece of avant-garde writing, the work of a nine-year-old author named Tony Lynott:

A THANKSGIVING STORY

Once upon a time there was a turkey. That turkey had an enemy. This enemy was a man. One day they had a fight and the man won.

THE END

I venture the opinion that this Tony Lynott is on his way to the literary heights. He's what we call stark. His Thanksgiving story has already appeared in a school publication and I think I'll preserve it as the first work of a youngster who may turn out to be the Hemingway of the 1970's.

A teacher in North Carolina has forwarded an exercise in logic written by a ten-year-old girl. It throws new light on the traffic problem. Here it is:

Don't stand around in the street. If everybody stood around in the street how would people get by?

From a rural school in Massachusetts comes a remarkable essay on a subject which is a favorite with many children. An eleven-year-old farm boy was given the assignment and produced the following:

The horse is the most useful animal in the world. So is the cow. I once had thirteen ducks and two was Drakes. I once knew a boy that had 7 chickens but his father woodent let him keep them so he got mad and bored a hole in his fathers wheelbare. My dog is named Rustey. We have two cats. I wish I had a horse. A horse weighs 1000 pounds.

I have no documentary evidence to support it, but I imagine that I wrote like that when I was eleven years old. I still do. I can almost always get a real interesting statement to start off with and I can almost always work out a real fascinating ending. But it's that middle part that proves troublesome. I'm just like that Massachusetts boy. If I'm writing about a horse, I start out real good, and then somehow I get all involved with cows and ducks and Drakes and chickens and wheelbares and dogs and cats, and then finally, sometimes, I manage to get back to the horse. Proust is the same way.

The public has always been amused by the spectacle of the city boy, especially the boy from New York City, who is transported suddenly to the rural districts.

Perhaps the most famous dispatch from a New

York City child, visiting on an upstate farm, was the letter he wrote home to his parents in which he said:

There were all these little pigs. They saw a great big pig and they chased him all around the pen and caught him and then threw him down on the ground and started chewing the buttons off his vest.

There are at least three candidates for the title of Youngest Poet.

Peggy Mann, author of the 1956 novel *A Room in Paris*, wrote a poem and had it published at the age of three. Actually she didn't write it, because she couldn't write, but dictated it to her mother and it was published in FPA's column, "The Conning Tower." It follows:

> When we dance round the Christmas tree,
> We are full of good glee.
> But those who have no Christmas tree,
> Haven't any good glee.

Frances Gray Patton also was three years old when she wrote her first poem. My source doesn't say she dictated it. It's a lovely thing, although members of the Audubon Society probably won't like it. Here it is:

The wind is blowing sofly
The birds are singing awfly.

Our third candidate is a male. It is well known that the female matures earlier than the male, even in poetry, hence Neill C. Wilson was all of four years old when he wrote:

Higgledy piggledy my black hen
She lays eggs for Jesus sake amen.

Great stacks of books have been written by people in an effort to explain why Rome fell. Scholarly historians have devoted their whole lives to the question, yet none of them ever really arrived at a more sensible answer than that contained in a penciled manuscript unearthed in Greenwich, Connecticut, one day in 1948. It was the work of a nine-year-old boy and follows:

THE DOWNFALL OF ROME
The Downfall of Rome was caused by carelessness.

That sapient bit of historical analysis found its way eventually into the pages of the *New Yorker*, a sort of clearing house for the finest writing produced by American children. Parents and teachers all over the land, whenever they come upon a bit of juvenilia which they consider pretty close to immortal, think immediately of the *New Yorker*. A parent in Indianapolis, for example, sent in an essay written on assignment by a seventh-grader, as follows:

WHY I WANT TO BE IN
THE EIGHTH GRADE

There are not many reasons why I want to be in the Eighth Grade.

And a nine-year-old boy won his first literary prize for the following composition:

MANNERS

I have good manners. I say good night and good morning and hello and goodbye, and when I see dead things lying around the house I bury them.

Fred Beck, the Los Angeles author, gourmet, golfer and radio wit, remembers a letter he wrote when he was six years old. It was, in fact, his first published work. His father was editor of a Montreal newspaper and when little Fred was taken for a visit to Detroit, his father urged that he send back a dispatch on the state of affairs in the Michigan metropolis. The following letter, which was published in the Montreal paper, was the result:

Dear Daddy
   Ty Cobb with the butcher had a fight I love you
Fred

Now in 1956 Fred Beck says he is confused by that letter. In a way I understand why. He says he is positive that it had meaning at the time he wrote it. It is a strange thing that a man with such a clear recollection of the exact wordage of the letter is, at the same time, so unclear about its meaning. "I was sober at the time," says Mr. Beck.

Well, I have tried to puzzle it out for him. It may be that he went to the ball park and witnessed an affair in which Ty Cobb got into a fight with a candy butcher. Or it may be that the fight took place in a butcher shop, over short-weighting or some such thing; if this were true, however, it seems likely that the Beck boy would have reported that Ty Cobb whipped a butcher, or a butcher whipped Ty Cobb. There is a third explanation, which I'm inclined to favor. Young Beck and another boy were walking along a Detroit street. They saw two men approaching. Little Fred spoke: "See that man

walking along with the butcher? That's Ty Cobb."
The other boy said, "It ain't either — you are a
Canuck liar." This intemperate remark led to a fight

between the two boys, not between Ty Cobb and
the butcher. Sounds *fairly* reasonable, doesn't it?

When Bennett Cerf's son Jonathan was eight
years old, he and his schoolmate Judy Goetz were
assigned to write a play. The first Mr. Cerf heard
of the project was when Judy stormed into his
house, complaining that the teacher had rewritten
the entire first scene of the drama. Mr. Cerf asked
if he might see the manuscript. The first scene, as
originally written, went this way:

[41]

The curtain rises. A frog is on the center of the stage.

Frog: I don't think I'll go to school today.

Curtain

Mr. Cerf says he never did find out what kind of editorial revision the teacher performed on that scene. It could be that she was afraid of frogs and arbitrarily changed the character from a frog to something else, say an armadillo. I prefer to believe that her revision was a trivial thing — that she simply cut out one word and had the frog say, "I think I'll go to school today."

While we're on theatrical matters, let's examine Katharine Cornell's first press notice. When she was a little girl her family had a summer home at Cobourg, Ontario. Katharine and her friends published one issue of a four-page newspaper, the Cobourg *Sun*. In that issue appeared the following review:

ACTING IS HARD

Katharine Cornell and Jo Pierce wrote an A–1 play called The Hidden Treasure. The editor played the part of the Duke. In one part where Katharine was on the stage and the curtain man was half asleep, she called out "Curtain, Curtain," which made the people laugh. We made 20 cents on the whole thing.

A twelve-year-old boy in one of the Mount Kisco schools recently handed in a poem which might be titled "The All-Inclusive Mother." It follows:

MY MOTHER

The most dainty butterflies
are not as dainty as you!
When it comes to opening stuck things
You are right there too.

We come now to the billing department. The *New Yorker* once reported on an eleven-year-old girl who had been escorting a neighbor's younger child to the Chapin School. The girl submitted her bill for services rendered as follows:

TO MRS. OR DR. WILLIAMS:

$1.50 per one month
$1.50 per 3/4 month
———
$3.00
  .50 cents for Nancy's bad behaveyer
  .50 cents more for Nancy's bad behaveyer again.
———
$4.00

I think this is fair, don't you? If not, I'll put it down lower.

Sincerely yours,
Cathy

Edward Weeks, editor of the *Atlantic Monthly*, admires an essay which he found in the works of Sir Ernest Gowers. A ten-year-old boy, told to write about a bird and a beast, produced the following:

The bird that I am going to write about is the Owl. The Owl cannot see at all by day and at night is as blind as a bat.

I do not know much about the Owl, so I will go on to the beast which I am going to choose. It is the Cow. The Cow is a mammal. It has six sides — right, left, upper and below. At the back it has a tail on which hangs a brush. With this it sends the flies away so that they do not fall into the milk. The head is for the purpose of growing horns and so that the mouth can be somewhere. The horns are to butt with, and the mouth is to moo with. Under the cow hangs the milk. It is arranged for milking. When people milk, the milk comes and there is never an end to the supply. How the cow does it I have not yet realized, but it makes more and more. The cow has a fine sense of smell; one can smell it far away. This is the reason for the fresh air in the country. The man cow is called an ox. It is not a mammal. The cow does not eat much, but what it eats it eats twice, so that it gets enough. When it is hungry it moos, and when it says nothing it is because its inside is all full up with grass.

A Nebraska schoolteacher instructed her pupils to write about the most exciting experience they had

had in the preceding week. One ten-year-old girl turned in a paper which the teacher forwarded to Walter Davenport of *Collier's*. Here it is:

VISTING OUR NEW NEIGHBORS

They are a family of four — two boys. The older is a schoolboy, the younger is still a playboy. They have bouncy pillows, an electric corn popper, the mamma has a run in her stocking, and they believe in Jesus.

Also from Mr. Davenport's files comes a superb short story produced by a nine-year-old lass of his acquaintance:

Once upon a time there was a little girl named Clarise Nancy Imogene Ingrid LaRose. She had no hair and rather large feet. But she was extremely rich and the rest was easy.

Joanna Espy wrote a short story when she was nine and this is the way it went:

CAROL'S CURCIS MONKEYS

Carol all ready had a horse a rabbit a dog and a cat but she wanted some monkeys. She told her parents but they said no but they decided they would surprize her on her birthday.

Meantime Carols Mother and father were looking for some monkeys, Carols father saw a pet shop and wanted to go in to see if there were any monkeys in it when they got inside it they ownly saw Monkeys and rabbits. A man came up and said can I help you. Carols father said yes were looking for a couple of monkeys that would be good for a ten year old child to play with. The man said the ownly Monkeys we have for a child is curcis monkeys that do a lot of tricks and there more trouble than just plane monkeys. Mr. Brown said how much do they cost, the other man whispered the a mount so that Mrs. Brown coudnt make any remarks about the cost or the money. Mr. Brown said he'd by the curcis Monkeys and that he wanted to pick them up the day before the childs birthday then they went home.

Joanna's mother, overlooking the slur on American womanhood, read this story and said she didn't think it had a proper ending; that Joanna should fetch it to an exciting climax by having Mr. Brown bring the curcis Monkeys home to Carol. Joanna disputed the need for a new ending. "Everybody knows already," she said, "how it comes out." This statement would seem to indicate that Joanna will go a long way as a writer.

Some years ago the Milwaukee *Sentinel* ran a contest in which children were to write letters on the subject "My Pop's Tops." Among the lovely entries were these:

We have such good fun with my daddy that I wisht I had knew him sooner.

He taked me fishin he taked me hunting, once he even taked me to the burlest show. It was wonderful.

He is a farmer. He smells like a cow and when I smell that cow in the house I know Pop is home and I am glad.

My Pop is tops because every time I ast him for a knickel he will start preeching that when he was a boy he had to earn his kenickls and at the same time he is puting his hand in his pocket and pulls out a kinckel, saying this is the last kinkel I have.

My Pop's tops because he was a brave soldier. He didn't see me until I was three years old yet he is just as good to me as if he knew me all my life.

Our next author is a precocious young incendiary named Jimmy. That is not his real name; his father has told me that if I use any real names in reporting this particular matter, he will punch me in the snoot. I am not one to be intimidated, so let's call the boy Jimmy and say that he attends a private school in Connecticut. The name of the school is Park Academy.

Jimmy is ten years old, a superior scholar and well behaved except for a tendency to set things on fire. His parents are unable to keep matches out of his hands. He has set his own house afire three times, burned down his father's tool shed, and started a grass fire that spread over several hundred acres before it could be stopped.

After a series of consultations the parents and the headmaster of Park Academy decided to try a psychological approach to the problem. The headmaster set the plan in motion. One day the pupils in Jimmy's class were told to write compositions on the subject "The Boy Who Started Fires."

As soon as all the papers had been turned in they were quietly shunted over to the headmaster's office. All of them, except Jimmy's, condemned the practice of arson by the young. One even went so far as to conclude: "Any boy that starts a fire ought to be burned up there self."

Jimmy's composition, however, was different. He had written:

THE BOY WHO STARTED FIRES

Once there was a boy who started fires. People put them out so he started some more. People put them out. One day he said he was sick because he had some matchs and couldent go to school. So he crep over to Park Academy and put some careseen on some rags and burnd the whole school up. Mr Carrol was burnd up & Mr Willims was burnd up also all the teachers but not Mr Peck the janiter all though he was badley scortched. It was very sad for some people.

The last I heard, nobody seems to know just what to do about Jimmy. I like to think that the headmas-

ter, after reading Jimmy's composition, went to the parents and said, "I hate to tell you this, but it looks very much as if your boy is going to grow up to be a humorist. Better start flogging him."

Ellery Sedgwick, the noted editor, remembers a childhood essay which he had to read aloud before a group of parents in the school he attended at Stockbridge. Here it is, complete:

THE OWRANG OWTANG

The owrang owtang is a very interestible animal.

As a child, Eudora Welty, author of *The Ponder Heart* and other stories, produced romantic tales in which the action usually took place in Paris. She recalls the opening lines of one such story:

Monsieur Boule deposited a delicate dagger in Mademoiselle's left side and departed with a poised immediacy.

The Thompsons of North Shoreland Avenue in Milwaukee treasure a short story written by daughter Joan when she was eight. Joan's mother admits that the child had been following the daytime serials on television and that there is a distinct soap-opera flavor to her script, which follows:

A SPLEDID WORKOUT FOR MARY

Once upon a time there was a girl named Mary, Mary was the kind that anyone wold like. She lived at 8363 North Hooly wood. phone number wo 2-3510. Mary had a very pretty house. One afternoon there

came a noak at the door when Mary opend it there
stood Nick the one she was engaged to. Nick said:
Mary there is something I have to tell you, Nick
stoped, well then dont just stand there say it. Mary
are egagedment is off Nick said. is it Judy the other
girl whoum you had a date with last night. No Nick
said I'm going to Boston. Boston cried Mary. But you
cant, yes I can said Nick. Well when are you going.
At four oclock today so I must get the packing done
now Good-by. Mary colsed the door and ran to the
tellaphone and said: operator get me the airport. Be-
couse Nick said he was going by plane. Well the oporator got her the airport. Hello Mary said when could
I get a reservesten, well said the voice we just got a call
for abenece of one for three pm to Boston is that O. K.
Fine said Mary and she hung up. Now to find out
were he is staying thought Mary. so up went the recver
of the phone and Mary said oporator give me wo 4-
6362. The oporator got the number and Nick ansered
and Mary said Nick were are you staying, at the Hotel
on 4th street room 44 Nick said. then he hung up.
Mary got the oporator, and she told her to get the
hotel. Mary got room 45 and so Nick and Mary got
Maried and lived happly ever after.

I am not a literary critic, so there are some things
I don't understand. One of them is the location of
that hotel. Is it in Boston, or somewhere else? And
if it's not in Boston, what happened to those airport reservations? Oh, well — we know that in lit-

erature what you don't write is often more important than what you do. Such as, was there a connecting door between Rooms 44 and 45 in that hotel?

The manner in which a poem is conceived is often important to the understanding of the work itself. Mrs. Paula R. Livesley tells us how her seven-year-old daughter appeared on the scene one morning with a poem which she had illustrated herself. But first, the poem:

A DOG'S LIFE

I'm a little dash hound
In a very little pound,
And all I can eat
Is a little piece of meat,
And perhaps a little milk
But I'd rather be an elk.

The drawing depicted a long dog, lying behind a fence, dreaming of an elk.

"I think the whole thing is lovely," said Mrs. Livesley, "but how did you come to write it?"

"Well," said her daughter, "I couldn't get to sleep last night because I had so much thinking to do, so I just thought and dreamed and thought and dreamed and pretty soon I had a poem all thought out."

I'm indebted to Mrs. Helen G. Sutin of Albany for the story of Patti and the spider. Mrs. Sutin's daughter, Patti, is ten and has a deep affection for those of Nature's children condemned to creep and crawl. Patti, in fact, has often been in trouble at school for bringing these creatures to class with her. Patti's teacher, Miss Hull, did not share the child's love for creepy-crawly things.

Then one day a spider appeared, crawling across another pupil's desk, and there was a momentary uproar. Patti had never seen the spider before, but since she was a friend and patron to spiders generally, she was blamed for introducing it into the classroom. She knew that it would be futile to deny the charge, so she held her tongue.

It happened, however, that the English assignment for the day followed immediately after the discovery of the spider. Patti applied herself to her composition. Then, perhaps as a form of punishment, Miss Hull called upon her to read her essay aloud to the class. Patti did read it, and she read it dramatically, placing strong emphasis on certain sentences, as follows:

A NEW PUPIL

One day, I was sitting in school doing my writing lesson, when I heard a gast from the back of the room. I turned around to see Maria Cutturini with her chair pulled away from her desk and a horrified look on her face. Then I saw the reason for her gast. Crawling over her writing book was a big yellow spider. I snatched out of my desk a little bag I happened to have and went to the recue. Miss Hull, our teacher thought the spider had run away from me because she knew how I love Insects. She said, "Why did you bring that spider to school?" I didn't have to answer because I *knew she knew that I brought him, even if I didn't bring him.* I decided that the spider had come to school to learn something but he didn't learn much in that little bag in which I carried him home!

Ah, the power of dramatic writing! Patti's essay restored her to high standing among her classmates, and Miss Hull . . . well, Miss Hull *smiled.*

I have examined a dozen or so compositions on the subject of Christopher Columbus, but the best of the lot was written by John Jacobson in the fourth grade at Rolling Green School in Rockford, Illinois. Here it is:

CHRISTOPHER COLUNBUS

Christopher Colunbus was the man who discovered America. Colunbus believed the earth a ball. He asked the king and Queen for ships. The king said "no"! For seven long years he asked and asked the king and Queen. One day the Queen called for Colunbus and said. "What do you need ships for? I want ships so I can go to India by going west. "no!" He asked and asked. One day the Queen said you may get ships. The ships are named the Nina Pinta and Santamaria. The next day Columbris was on the dark sea. Weeks and weeks they sailed. One day a man saw land and they landed. The people were red and so Colunbris named the people Indians. The Santamaria was wrecked. So the Nina and Pinta went back to Spain.

In his life he made 4 voyages and on the last voyage he went back with a stiffening of the joints and died.

This same boy, John Jacobson, turned out another essay which I find both entertaining and informative:

WHY I THINK THE SWISS GO DOWN THE MOUNTAIN IN WINTER.

They go down because the hut will cave in from the snow. The cow will die and you will freeze.

Advanced biology is not ordinarily taught in the second grade. Yet there are strong biological overtones to an essay written by Sanford Rosenberg some years ago in the second grade of a Buffalo school. Sanford's composition was preserved by his teacher, Miss Freda H. Meyer, and follows:

[55]

THE NEST

Theres a nest outside Miss Lodges window and some bird eggs are there. The mother robin is sitting on the eggs. Soon the eggs will hatch and out will come the baby robins. Then mother and father robin will have to feed their babys with lots of worms and keep

them warm. When the baby robins grow up they to will lay eggs. Thats how bird life goes. Our life is different. Your mother doesnt go to market to buy some eggs and go home and then sit on them till they hatch your baby brother or sister. No she goes to the hospital.

Mrs. E. O. Adler has sent me a horror story composed by her young daughter. On the basis of her first effort, I think the young lady will grow up to achieve fame and fortune as a writer of TV scripts. Turn the lights low now and read:

"THE NOVEMBER NIGHT"

It was a dark, cloudy November night, when I Daisy Dinkle appeared on the scene. I had been over my mom's barn to pitch hay, when all of a sudden a figure appeared.

This frighten me to know end. For I had know idea as to what this man wanted from me. Wheather to murder or to rob me of my money.

All I heard as I walked down the cobblestone street was echoing footsteps. At first I thought they were my own, but I found out they wern't.

It was a very dark night I couldn't see in front of me. So I didn't see this figure approach me with a lighted cigarette. He drew blood from my neck. Later I learned that this someone was a firebug, not only did I have a sizzling neck from that terrifying burn, my neck was dripping with blood.

I couldn't understand why, or with what reason this someone would want to burn me. I tried to reason out why this person would try a thing like that.

Still I made up my mind to find out more about this person, no matter how I had to. This was just the beginning.

One day, while I was crossing the street a car drove in front of me. I began to tremble, thinking about my burn.

There were several more attempts. For instance, the time I was in the front room watching television, and I heard a noise. I was scared stiff I was afraid to move. I turned around and there was a man with a gash three inches long on his cheek to his chin. He was horrid looking. One side of his face was puffed out, he had frog eyes, rotten teeth, he was at least two hundred pounds. You've never seen any one as ugly as he. His next attempt was to try me again. Well, this was the forth time. I was in bed, when all of a sudden, I heard a noise. I got scared on account of the other times. On the other side of my door was that horrifying face. It scared me so, I shook in my slippers.

I stuck a chair under the door. While I was asleep, he finally opened the door he came toward's me with a lighter. He burned my face very badly. I suffered pains of the burns, I was scared for life. The man who ever he was or what ever he wanted, he must had gotten his wish. He was caught by one of the tenants while running in the hall, he had heard Daisy Dinkle scream and come rushing out. The police took care of him, but good Ol' Daisy was his first victim.

The police told me his name was George Brent. He loved the gleam of fire. When he was a shafer he stole matches. Also, when he was three he burned his sister's nose to a crisp.

THE END

Seven-year-old Charlotte McNiel of Windsor, Ontario, produced an entire novel in a single afternoon. She kept popping out of her room, asking

[58]

how to spell certain words, and finally she emerged
with her finished work. It had been printed on cardboard sheets, taken from her father's shirts, and
these boards were fastened together with bits of
string. On the front cover Charlotte had pasted a

picture depicting the beauty of family life; this picture may have furnished a clue to the moral of her
story, which follows:

THE MAN THAT DID WRONG

There was a man who lived near by a psychiatrist.
He hated him. There was a girl who loved him deadly.
The Quakers were living peaceably. One day the psychiatrist came with a needle. It was full of poison. He
pulled the man and gave him a needle. He died in
three minutes. They soon caught him. Soon they were
in the court room. Carelessly the judge left the window open. Just then a big pig jumped through the win-

dow. The pig jumped up on the judges lap and laid down.

Then the pig began to snort. On Thanksgiving the Quakers had a indigestible meal. The man they caught was not the real man. On Thanksgiving the wrong man was executed. The mother saw him and began to cry.

When the girl saw him she began to cry too. Soon he was dead and they buried him. Every night he would haunt the psychiatrist. And he would carry a lamp in his hand and said I hate you.

Grown-up novelists will recognize at least one important technical device in Charlotte's novel. It comes at the point where the judge carelessly left the window open. I was reading along, hair on end, fully expecting the Quaker man, or the psychiatrist, or whoever it was, to make a wild leap for that open window and escape. Instead, a big pig jumped *in*. Folks, that's writin'!

Phyllis McGinley has become one of the nation's most popular poets. She has written several volumes of verse, but of all her work I think I like best the poem she turned out when she was six years old. It does something to me. Here it is:

> Sometimes in the evening
> When the day is red and pink

I love to lie in a hammock
And think and think and think.

The art of poetry has always been considered the most difficult of writing forms, but, as we have already seen, it is not difficult for children. Where an adult might very well labor for weeks or even months over a single sonnet, a child sits down and knocks off a poem with all the facility he might employ in eating a banana.

Jean Stafford, whose present-day fiction is considered to be of exceptional quality and loaded with hidden meanings, produced a poem at the age of six. It follows:

Gravel, gravel on the ground,
Lying there so safe and sound,
Why is it you look so dead?
Is it because you have no head?

I am not very good at hidden meanings and I don't know what the hidden meanings are in that poem, but I suspect there are some. After giving considerable thought to it, I find that it says something to me. It tells me that I am extremely fortunate that gravel has no head. (Jean Stafford, by the way, says that when she was a little girl she read quite a bit in the newspapers, and for a long while she thought that one of the crimes for which people were arrested was man's laughter.)

Another child poet to consider is Mary Small. Years ago when I was a newspaper interviewer I had a long talk with Miss Small, then a prominent juvenile singing star. At the time of the interview she was sixteen and she said she could remember writing a poem when she was eight, a poem called "My Dad." I asked her if she could recite it, and she could and she did. I copied it down as follows:

MY DAD

He's the best in the world
And will always be,
One dad, only one,
Will there be for me.
He works and toils
And never complains.
But secretly inside
Endures his pains.
We greet him with joy
When he comes home at night,
From his labors to home
Is a wonderful sight.
When he plays with us
We have such fun

For he loves his two daughters
And his dear little son.
We'll worship him
Through sorrow and tears,
And I'll work for him
For the rest of my years.

I was much younger then than I am now, and
more romantic in my outlook, and I must confess
that I was stirred by Miss Small's poem. I told her
it sounded beautiful but that there was one part
that didn't quite mesh — the part where it says,
"From his labors to home is a wonderful sight."

"Just *what* is a wonderful sight, Mary?" I asked
her.

"From his labors to home is a wonderful sight,"
she said, her blue eyes getting very wide.

"Yes," I said, "that's what it says in the poem,
but it doesn't sound right."

"I know it doesn't," she agreed, "but that's the
way I wrote it. I was very corny in those days."

I think you'll search a long time before you find
a grown-up poet who will confess to being confused
by his own stuff. I don't think T. S. Eliot would
ever unbend and make such an admission as Miss
Small made. And I doubt that T. S. Eliot talks
much about *his* first venture into writing. When he

was seven years old he wrote a two-page biography of George Washington. The last line of it was:

And then he died, of corse.

T. S. Eliot was very corny in those days.

Sage advice is to be found in the following essay, written by Freddy Espy at the age of ten:

HOW TO BEHAVE IN THE LIBRARY

When you walk into the libray you should be quite. There might be people reading, Tring to do a report and a number of differant things. Even if nobodys working its not polite to run in and talk loudly. Another thing is its not polite to chew gum in the library.

When you go around looking for books you shouldn't slam them around in and out of the shelves. You should be quite in the library at all times.

Once upon a time there was a fabulously prosperous period in the book-publishing business. Everything was selling. Anything was selling. Along came a publisher with an idea. He had a famous author write the first chapter of a novel. Another famous author wrote the second chapter. Then the manuscript was passed along to a third famous author and he wrote his chapter. And so on, to the end.

If memory serves, the book sold like atomic reactors.

The same idea was employed not long ago at Whittier, California. A grade-school teacher had her pupils write a story, the title and each succeeding sentence being contributed by a different youngster. Mrs. M. F. Warner of Whittier has sent along the result, which follows:

SANDY THE BUZZARD

Once there was a buzzard.

His name was Sandy.

One day when he was flying he smelled a dead dog.

He went down and took a look at him.

A good look, too.

It smelled real good.

The buzzard said, "He sure looks good lookin'!"

And he started eating it.

He ate it until he came to a bone.

Then he couldn't eat any more because it was now a skeleton.

He smelled another dead animal so he went down there.

He said, "What is that?"

It didn't smell so good and he found out it was a skunk.

Next he came to a dead pigeon.

He thought the material was good and he made a coat with it.

There was some left over and he made a rug.

Then he decided he would fly away.

He flew back to his nest.

He had brought some pieces of meat back for his little buzzards but they said it was no good.

But the mother made them eat it.

So they would grow up to be big buzzards.

The teacher said she contributed nothing to this story "except the elimination of astounding words." I can't think of any astounding words that would fit into it, except maybe "Yurp!"

Fred Beck thinks I should not overlook the occasional excellence of compositions written in wet cement. A sidewalk on South Barrington Avenue in Los Angeles is boldly inscribed with:

WE DID THIS JUNE 4 1955

The pupils in Mrs. Miller's class at Hamburg, New York, had been studying Greek mythology. Eventually they were set to work composing their own myths.

Here is what Karen Markley wrote:

ZEUS AND HIS PET ANT

Many centuries ago Zeus came down from the sky. He brought his pet ant along with him to the earth. Zeus let the ant crawl along the ground. Suddenly the ant fell into a deep pit. This angered Zeus, so he pulled a tree out of the earth. Then he took a flat rock and fastened it to the tree. Zeus dug into the ground and chased the little ant all the way around the world.

Finally he gave up hope. Then Hera, queen of heaven, sent gallons of water down from the sky. Zeus was getting worried. He looked about him and saw canyons and valleys. One valley was over two hundred thousand miles wide. So he climbed the highest mountain of dirt. Soon the valleys and canyons were filled with water. Then Poseidon came down from the sky and dove into the water. Ever since then he was called god of the sea.

As for the ant. He met another ant and they multiplied.

Twenty years ago the seven-year-old son of a prominent political figure in Washington spent his summer vacation on a small farm in Maryland. From this experience, it was hoped, he would grow up to understand all about parity, flexible price supports, and sitch. His first letter home follows:

Dear Mom & Dad

Everything is all right on the farm. We go in town to the show. We went to the show intending to see Alexander Gram Bell but saw Susanh of the Mountains Surly Tempel. Mirs. Kenny said Surly is getting to fat. Wensday we are going to see Vern & Iren Casle. I am red as a apple from sun burn and get up at 530 every morning. Henry milks the cow and I spray it with fly spray. Wish you were here.

Dave.

Ps. We had a wheeny rost.

One of the most glittering performances in the field of historical romance was the work of Peter Matson. Back in 1943, when he was eight, Peter turned out a swashbuckling saga of "the olden time" and titled it *The Box That Wouldn't Open*. His father, Norman Matson, a writer of fiction, thought that Peter's work had merit and showed it around and a national magazine bought it and published it.

A dozen years have passed since Peter wrote his story. It is no longer much remembered as a story, but a tiny part of it has achieved a sort of immortality. Somewhere in the tale was the line:

Useless to talk, said the French spy.

That line became common currency in the Norman Matson household, as it still is. Whenever any troublesome situation arises and it can't be resolved by sober discussion, someone in the family will finally shrug and say, "Useless to talk, said the French spy." The very speaking of the line usually restores good humor and clears the atmosphere, and the problem at hand is quickly solved. The practice of quoting it has spread through the years to the families of relatives and friends until nowadays it is heard frequently in various parts of our country and in foreign lands. It has brought a happy conclusion to many a quarrelsome interlude and for that reason I think it's an important contribution to literature — a more worthwhile piece of writing, perhaps, than *Rebecca of Sunnybrook Farm*.

Ten-year-old Connie La Butte of Detroit enjoys playing "Doctor and Nurse." Recently her mother came upon the following document:

APOINTMENTS

Today.
Mrs. Barker — Heart Attack
Mr. Smith — Nervous type
Carole Steinfelt — Tonculs out
Mrs. La Butte — having a baby
Mr. Nickerson — T–B
Connie La Butte — glans out
6 o'clock tomorrow night
Mrs. York — Cancer
Sandra Amati — Heart is bad
Mr. Paul — appendix out

It looks very much as if Connie, in the role of doctor, is going to take her own glans out the day after delivering her mother's new baby.

The Elisha story has become a classic in the field of preadolescent writing. The identity of the author is unknown, but this is what he wrote in Sunday school:

Once there was a man named Elisha. He owned three bears and they lived in a dark cave. One day some little boys threw stones at Elisha and Elisha said, If you throw stones at me, I'll tell my bears and they'll eat you up. And they did and he did and the bears did.

I've checked this version with the original in the Second Book of Kings. The facts have been altered somewhat, but the little boy's story reads easier, and has more drama and flair to it.

Equally graphic is the Noha story, written by nine-year-old Jay Miles of New Orleans, and sent to me by his aunt:

NOHAS ARK

Once opon a time there was a man caled Noha and he said God told him there was going to be a flood for forty day and nights. All of the animals were scared, Noha said that he would build an ark and flot it on the water. All of the animals were woried what would they eat on the ark. Noha said that his three sons had been gathering food for days. And then it was decided two of each kind of animals was to go. The next day it started to get cold and then it started to rain and then all the animals started to run for the ark and Noha got all of animals on the ark and they started to sail they sailed for a long time all of a sudden the ark

started to tare apart and all of the animals and Noha came tumbleing out of the ark all of the animals and Noha grabed pieces of wood the animals became resles after a while the red cross came and saved them.

Eleven-year-old Margaret Morkill of Calgary, Canada, was proud of her father that day when he came home from the golf course with the big news. Margaret decided to celebrate the achievement in verse and turned out the following:

HOLE IN ONE

H. S. Morkill scored an ace.
It was a great race.
To see who would suceed it first.
Every man and woman cursed.
Because it came to H. S. first.
He won a cup that caused a great thrill
For dear old H. S. Morkill.
H. S. Gillies, Eric Richardson, Norman Hanley played
    with him.

Some of the rhythmic perfection of the poem is destroyed by that last line, but I suppose Margaret felt that witnesses were important.

One of the most widely quoted bits of preadolescent writing is a letter from a ten-year-old girl to a children's book club. The club had sent the child a volume about penguins, enclosing a card urging her to express her opinion of it. She wrote:

This book gives me more information about penguins than I care to have.

The late Hugh Gibson, who served both the government and the book world, described that letter as the finest piece of literary criticism he had ever read.

An eight-year-old girl in a New York school handed in a composition describing the automobile trip she had taken with her family to Niagara Falls. The concluding sentence follows:

On the way home we past through many lovely fallen rock zones.

It took a child to recognize a fact that was never apparent to me: if you can keep your mind off getting hit by a boulder, a fallen rock zone is almost always lovely.

Hollywood's major contribution to this collection was first printed by Erskine Johnson. The young daughter of a movie producer was told in school to write a story about a poor family. This is how she did it:

Once upon a time there was a poor family. The mother was poor. The daddy was poor. The children were poor. The butler was poor. The chauffeur was poor. The maid was poor. The gardener was poor. Everybody was poor.

According to the *New Yorker* a young mother found some wadded balls of paper in the wastebasket. They turned out to be the beginnings of stories written by her eight-year-old daughter. One of them read:

Humphry Mandelbaum looked at the bloody corps and urped.

From the same magazine's accumulation of camp letters comes one written by a boy to his mother. It is a penciled three-page letter of personal and camp trivia, and a fourth page covered with a variety of hieroglyphics, including X's under the notation:

This page reserved for kisses and other flap-doodle.

The delights and excitements of camp life, in fact, have produced so many literary treats that making selections from among them becomes a difficult problem. One of my favorites, written by a girl attending a camp in the Adirondacks, goes like this:

Dear Mom & Daddy

Our counclor is swell but a little cracked she was adobted by the Indians and lived with them a while. Wah-loo-lah-wah is her Indian name. She doesnt really wear a feather & she doesnt look like an indian except for her pig-tails. We killed 2 baby mouse this morning.

Love,

Joanne.

Further proof that unfinished manuscripts are often more thought-provoking than those that have been brought to an adequate conclusion is evident in a "book" by six-year-old Douglas Broder of Shaker Heights, Ohio. The entire manuscript follows:

THIS IS A BOOK ON THINGS THAT ARE RIGHT

You should pet your dog when you get home from school but should not come home and slap your dog and the same with your kitten.

That's as far as Douglas got with it. My guess is that he ran into a "writer's slump" and couldn't think of any other things that are right. If some other author knows about a lot of things that are right, I'm sure Douglas would permit the use of his title . . . provided he got a share in the royalties.

Margaret Whiting, the classy singer, remembers a poem composed by her younger sister, Barbara. When Barbara was six, Margaret was just starting her career as a singer. Barbara simply couldn't stom-

ach all that attention Margaret was getting. One night there was a party at the Whiting home and after a while little Barbara was told to go to bed. She stomped off and the party continued. Margaret was in the middle of a song when Barbara appeared in the doorway and flung her poem into the room. It read:

> I Hate Margaret
> She'd make a good target
> She sings she thinks

But I think she stinks.
I Hate Margaret.

That poem was sent to me by Margaret and when I acknowledged it I suggested that Barbara's rhyming was bad. I said that if an Ogden Nash had written that verse, he'd probably have started off with:

> I Hate Margaret
> She'd make a good targaret.

Promptly came a letter from Barbara herself, defending her poem. She said that when she was six years old she pronounced her sister's name "Marget" and, therefore, "target" rhymed perfectly. Never criticize a poet's poetry.

In the fifth grade of a primary school in Knoxville it is the custom, at the beginning of each term, for the pupils to elect a class leader. It is also customary for the loser in the election to write a congratulatory message to the winner on the blackboard. Last year's loser wrote as follows:

Dear Class:
I congratulate Mildred Stokes on her election as the class leader. She is a much better one for leader than I am. Fooey.

Priscilla Caulkins.

Mrs. Mabel Hawkins teaches at the famous Little Red School House in New York City and she has saved hundreds of compositions turned in by her pupils. In common with many other educators Mrs. Hawkins believes that teachers and parents can learn from a child's writing a great deal about his personality and his problems. At the same time she recognizes the amusing quality that appears so often in the compositions.

Here are five samples of what children write about their parents:

My mother is always on the phone gabbing with another mother. She goes out about every night. And I always am practicing piano and sweat blood.

When I have been bad my mother says that I can't look at TV. My father always says that I won't do it again. And Mom gets mad at my father and forgets about me. Then I go ahead and look at TV while my father and Mom argue.

I like almost everything in dime stores. But as soon as I get ready to buy a few things my mother drags me out. My mother and I never agree on anything. In the morning I comb my hair — my mother doesn't like it, so she combs it over. Then she goes back to bed. Then I comb my hair again and go to school.

My parents are sometimes good and sometimes bad. My ma is quite fat, and she hates my bunny. She's always getting headaches and is quite a nuisance to have around. She always tells me to get out from under her feet when I'm not under her feet at all. My dad never laughs at a joke and is a nuisance to have around. Like all fathers he's too strict for his own good. So as I look at it there's no use for parents.

My father had soup on his vest one night and then there was a big fight. My mother and father were going out and my father stayed home because of the soup on his vest, which he wouldn't change, and because my mother opened her big fat jaws. I think my mother yells at me at the most unnecessary times . . . she can't wait to get home — oh no, she does it right in the store. I also think she chews too loud. I never get any peace at dinner time. Sometimes she's been nice to me all day and I think I could never be mad at her, when she starts slurping and chomping and I get so mad I could explode.

Also from Mrs. Hawkins's collection is this item:

IF I WERE PRESIDENT

If I were president I would be very mean. I would make everybody work very hard. I wouldn't let them build any new buildings, or any modern machinery, or anything new. But I would have everything I wanted.

A gentleman of my acquaintance, quite prominent in the radio and television business, suffered a slight embarrassment when his seven-year-old son Jonathan brought home a classroom composition. It read:

MY FATHER GOES ON A TRIP

My father had to go on a trip to Chicago and I helped him pack his bag. We put in the bag a pair of pajamas, a toothbrush and a quort of whiskey.

Jonathan's teacher, in a bold hand, had written across the top of this little essay:

"A" for Jonathan.
"D" for his father.

The home-published mimeographed newspaper has become a fairly common institution all over the land. Among those I've had the pleasure of examining is the Grove Beach *Report*, a Connecticut weekly. Its editor is Evelyn Linda Lanham, whose father is the novelist Edwin Lanham. Following are some typical items from this courageous journal:

BIRTHDAY

Jennifer Martin was 3 months old Friday and she almost turned over by herself in her crib.

SEAWALL REPAIRED

Topper McMillin and his cousin Dave Hinkley from Holyoke, Mass., repaired winter brakes of Fred Barhof's sea wall. Mr. Barhof had a seawall repairing party but everyone drank beer instead.

BICYCLE STOLEN

Some boys really showed how mean they could be last week when they stole Trenwith Ward's bike and of all the mean pranks they played the meanest.

It is well known how badly Trenwith catches poisen Ivey just a short while ago Trenwith had it very badly on his face. His whole face swelled up and he had to go to the doctors for it, it lasted several days.

The mean prank they played was to hide the bike in a poisen Ivy patch which you have probably all guessed, with both tires flat. It all took place on Tuesday. Friday Mr. Dana found it in this bad condition with poisen Ivy all over it.

TORNADO AT WORCESTER

Miss Judith Ann Solias has just returned from Worcester and this is her report of what she saw.

Where Carl Floodman works in Norton griding machin co. the roof blew in and the debreeze went 17 blocks the man that worked with Mr. Carl Floodman went flying through the air about 2000 ft. above the ground and his refrigerator just missed him. When he came to he found himself 7 blocks away from his home. The matter took place in 7 seconds. Miss Judy

Solias had the experience of speaking to a man whose home was split in to.

DYING WHITEFISH

There have been seen many dead whitefish washed up on the beach. It has been said that they have a sickness of the gills wich causes them to lose their balance and come to the top of the water wich more or less wakes them up and makes them struggle to get down again and they succeed to get down and they relax wich makes them come up again and they repeat the same process and so they don't see where they're going and get washed into shallow water and then they die. The Grove Beach cats go around picking them up.

The only home-published newspaper to which I am a subscriber is the *Fenelon Place Journal*. Its editor is Tom Bissell and it is published out of an establishment called Toad Hall at Rowayton, Connecticut (Editor Bissell is the son of author-playwright Richard Bissell). If the *Fenelon Place Journal* had covers on it, I would read it from cover to cover. As it is I prefer its editorial content to many of the professional journals that come to my house. By special permission, granted under the copyright regulations of the Berne Convention's Additional Protocol (1914), I offer a single contribution from its pages:

MY TRIP TO NEW YORK

By Stasie Bissell (Age 7½)

Tom and I got on the train at Darien at noon on Friday the 29th. We were going to New York! We were going to meat Father at grand sentral station. He took us to see "The Toy Tiger" at the Palace Theater and a lot of acts. There was a man with a fiddle, and a singer, and a shooting act, a migishun, a joke teller, Mizzy's Can Can Girls, and jugglers. In the migishun's act a dog jumped out of a pot. Then we went to Sis and saw her little TV set. Then Father took us to the Tavern on the Green. We ate and saw sky-writing. It said BATTER. We saw horse and buggys going past about thirty-three times. Tommy got me an old chewed-up comic to read on the train home. We had a keen time. THE END.

It seems to me that when I was a child the kids, like Mark Twain's Digger Indians, would eat anything they could bite. Things ain't like they used to be. Judging from their writing, the children of to-day are real picky about their food. I'm even informed that three-year-old Candace Olson of Minneapolis, when called upon to say grace at table, bowed her head and said, "Thank you, God, for our food, our tatuhs, fish and vegedubbles, but I don't like um."

The *New Yorker* has published several camp letters which touch on the matter of eating. One of these, from a nine-year-old boy vacationing in Virginia, follows:

Dear Mother:
Today I ate a snake. How are you?
Love, Robert.

That boy is plainly old-fashioned. He doesn't need to say so outright, but he'd eat anything. He ate a snake, and he liked it, else he'd have said it wasn't good. There are only two kinds of food to children — good and bad. If it's good, they don't say anything, they just eat it. If it's bad, they complain. As in this note:

Dear Mom and Dad,
The school is O. K. The masters are O. K. Only thing is the food. Its so bad I have gnawsher all the time.
Love, Dickie.

And still another from the files of the *New Yorker*:

Dear Aunt Frieda:
I am feeling fine. Hope you are the same. Camp is O. K. The food is wonderful, and they don't make you eat it.
Susan.

I may have placed the wrong interpretation on Susan's letter. Some people probably think she's a good eater. I don't. I think she's just being polite, showing her aunt how well she's been trained to always say that the food is wonderful. The key to her real thought lies in the line "and they don't make you eat it." If the truth were known, I think she also had gnawsher.

The importance of provender is emphasized in a brilliant essay sent to me by a schoolteacher in Dover, Delaware. It was written by an eight-year-old boy, possibly with his tongue in his cheek, and follows:

RULES FOR GOOD HEALTH

Dont climb on telaphone poles as you will get grounded and shocked and fall off. Dont eat anything in the medisin cabnet that has bones on it. Allways put idine in cuts. Dont hang on a brige. Eat all the food your mother gives you. The more you dont like a thing the gooder it is for you.

Many people have been put to sleep by a recording secretary reading the minutes of the last meeting. It takes a special sort of talent to "write up" the proceedings so that they sound lively and dramatic. I think Mona Espy has that talent. When she was eleven she served as a club secretary and her first report follows:

AUDABON MEETING

1 Meeting April 10, 1953.

We started are meeting off by Pam — president was showing us pictures of animals in North America. We tried to name the different animals of North America. Joey quit the club. We made rules for the club then we tried to see all the animals that we could out of are window. It was a rainy day so we couldn't see many. I saw a cat and herd some bird. then we named the animals of North America again at least tried to.

Every time I read through that report I grieve that fate didn't let me attend that meeting. And that, I think, is one of the chief reasons for having a good recording secretary — to make absentees sorry they missed all the fun. I'd have enjoyed being there just for that part of the meeting in which Joey quit the club. I'll bet it didn't happen quietly and it may be that things were thrown.

Agnes Andrews of Pittsburgh once taught a class of third-graders in a small West Virginia town. Among her pupils was a boy who, she firmly believes, will grow up to become either a Nobel Prize

[87]

winner in literature or President of the United States. Miss Andrews has sent me one of his compositions, which follows:

MY EASTER VACATION

During my Easter vacation there is a mean old man that lives on grover street and hides behind bushs. When we go to get the ball that goes there he jumps out and says get the h off my property or Ill have you sent to the pentensury. So we threw the ball on his property and he said get the h off my property and I said give me back my property meening my ball or Ill have you sent to the pentensury. so he gave it back. I had my tonsils out. Easter vacation can be a lot of fun if everybody takes care of theirself.

From a mountain of manuscripts I have plucked a single sheet that has me confused. It is, I suspect, the beginning of a thrilling novel, but the name of the author is not on it and I can't remember where it came from. The handwriting is ferociously bad, but this adds a good deal to the suspense of the tale. I have had to stop and puzzle out a word or two when my mind was simply screaming for me to get on to the next sentence. Anyway, bad handwriting doesn't indicate lack of genius. We know that some of Napoleon's affectionate letters to Josephine were taken to be rough maps of the seat of war.

Here, then, is the unidentified manuscript which, for all I know, may be one of the Dead Sea Scrolls:

I WORSHIP YOU

Chapter one

The weeds moved slightly. An Indian crept along cruching closer and closer to the recked plane. All of a sudden he turned around and beconed to someone. A whole groope of Indins then appered waving theire spears wildily. What this Golden bird that come out of sky? him say. The leader said to cut of metel. make plenty good spear heads. Just then a tribes man gave a scream. look in the rocks he cried pointing to a hollow place near the plane. Their in it was a small girl. Mabe she a god and is to curse our tribe for taking her great golden bird he exclamed.

I don't suppose any of us will ever find out if she was.

One of the few examples of genuine satire that has come my way is a poem written by Gary Johnson of Verona, N. J., when he was eleven. In order to recognize the satire, it is necessary to know that one of Gary's teachers was a Mr. Wilson. For some unexplained reason Gary bore a strong grudge against this Mr. Wilson and it is reflected in his poem, which follows:

THE BAKER OF BREAD

In olden days when you couldn't buy bread,
A man named Wilson galiently said,
I'll start a bakery and Ill bake the bread,
Some people said they'd rather not get fed.

Well he started a bakery and he baked the bread,
And a lot of people didn't get fed,
And even more got sick in the head,
All because of that baker of bread.

A man called the King ate some of this bread,
And two minutes later fell down, he was dead,

So all the knights, dressed up in lead,
Set out to find this baker of bread.

When Wilson heard this, he turned and fled,
He wound up in China but he wasn't dead,
He went to a doctor who simply said,
You just weren't made for baking bread.

So back to his country went this baker of bread,
And all the people happily said,
Since you baked this bread that made our king dead,
Were going to make you eat some of that bread.

So they opened his mouth and they shoved back his
    head,
And they took a long stick and they shoved down the
    bread,
And within 2 minutes he was deader than dead
He was out of his misery that baker of bread!

A teacher in Pensacola asked her pupils to write about a friend. One little boy turned in an essay which, among other reasons, is remarkable for the coinage of a brand-new verb. Here it is:

GORGE THE MECANIC

Gorge the mecanic at the garage is my friend. He lets me watch him fix cars. He says all boys ought learn how to fix cars so when they grow up he wont have to fix any and can retire to fish. When there is a rattle in the hood you take a peice of rubber with adheesive on it and stick it on and it adhees. This fixs it.

The sixth-graders at Laurelhurst School, according to the Seattle *Times*, were set to work writing autobiographies. When the teacher was correcting the paper submitted by Bruce Mowat, she found the following:

A funny experience I had when I was younger was when I took a roll of cardboard from the center of a roll of paper towels and buried it.

When my mother asked me why I did it, I told her I did it so the worms could crawl in it and shake the dirt off themselves.

Children are attracted to murder and mystery, the same as adults. The following tale, by ten-year-old Jay Miles, has a somewhat confusing title, but then the story itself is somewhat confusing!

DAILY BLADE

MASS MURDER

French Scientist Pierre' Duval Was murdered in his home last night at about 10:45 P. M. Police can't find the murderer. Duval was brought to the morgue this morning. Coroner's report said his spine was broken, it looks like some of the Creepers work says Police chief Henderson. If it is the Creepers work I'm

[92   ]

staying out of dark alleys. You never know when the Creeper will strike next. Police were supposed to have killed the creeper, when they shot him he fell in the water, but they never found his body, he must have recovered from the wound, or maybe they never shot him at all. Well all this beats me, I for one sure hope it isn't the creeper. It took five shots to get him once and he recovered, of course it has been two years, I guess with a good doctor, but what I can't understand is just who would treat the creeper. Police found footprints leading to the river, do you suppose it's the creepers ghost, well I guess nobody knows, if it is the creeper, just what motive would he have. Inspector Henderson says "and I quote" We'll get the creeper if its the last thing I do. And it just might be Inspector. As the police went Back to the sciene of the crime they found the hat and coat of the creeper.

More straightforward is the murder story found in an English book, a first-rate example written by a small boy, as follows:

CHAPTER I

There was once a merderer with yellow eyes and his wife said to him, If you merder me you will be hung. And he was hung on Tuesday next.

Finis

Some years ago Vincent Starrett, the Chicago littérateur and bibliophile, startled the world of letters with an astonishing discovery. Mr. Starrett, exploring in remote Winnetka, Illinois, stumbled upon the Sheerluck Hums papers.

These literary treasures turned out to be the work of Larry Yust, the young son of Walter Yust, editor of the *Encyclopaedia Britannica*. Beginning when he was eight or nine years old, Larry had written a whole series of stories about Sheerluck Hums, under such titles as *Sheerluck Hums and the Blushing Pigeon*, *Sheerluck Hums and the Mistery of the Lost Appetite*, and *Sheerluck Hums and the Missing Gold Tooth*.

We have space here for only a sampling of Larry Yust's graceful prose. This is the opening of one story, written at the age of nine:

There was a frantic knock at the door of the great Sheerluck Hums. Rat tat tat and double tat! What could that be, mused the great detective. Come in, he said in a quiet voice. A small man with a long beard burst through the door. He was very excited, his beard stood on end, pointing south. Mr. Hums, he gasped. Mr. Hums, the governor has lost his shirt. It must be found. We are getting well into the winter. The governor catches cold easily. His shirt must be found. Calm yourself, my good man, said Sheerluck Hums, picking his teeth, we'll find the governor's shirt.

A teacher in a Richmond school decided to test the descriptive powers of her English pupils. She placed an assortment of hardware on a table and instructed the children to choose any two items and describe them in an essay. One little girl's choice:

NUT AND BOLT

A bolt is a thing like a stick of hard metal such as iron with a square bunch on one end and a lot of scratching wound around the other end.

A nut is similar to the bolt only just the opposite being a hole in a little chunk of iron sawed off short with wrinkles around the inside of the hole.

These are times of compatible color and Cinemascope and VistaVision, but our children still have the urge to produce and stage their own circuses. One such show was put on last summer by a group of girls who spent upwards of three weeks in rehearsals and other preparations. John Ringling North would have admired the careful attention the girls gave to detail. Every move that was made in the whole performance was set down on paper ahead of time by one of the girls. She spent days typing out the directions for the parade, the dog-and-cat acts, the Oriental dances and so on. The careful thought that went into the whole production may be seen in the following description of one act:

TRICK ACT

Helen and Marty and I come out and stand. Then I get on my hands and knees and Helen gets on and stands. Then Marty gets on and stands, and points her toes. Then Helen gets on and I crawl and turn around and crawl back to the same place with out Helen falling off. Then Marty just gets on and stands. Then she gets on without holding on. Then Helen gets on and points her toe. Then I walk up to the door with Marty and Helen and I get on my hands and knees, then Marty and Helen get on my back and jump off and close the doors.

Part 2

Debbie does a row of summer sults, and then quitly runs off stage. Then Sharon runs and does a tummer sult, and after she runs jumps and does a tummer sult. Then Helen stands on her head. Then after she stands on her head, she stands on her head again only she does the split then points her toe then goes to the ground again. Then Sharon stands on her head and crosses her knee then Marty stands on her head and does the split. Then she stands on her head and points her toe to her knee. Then Helen stands on my knees holding on to my hands then she stands on my knees with out holding on to my hands. Then Sharon stands on my knees first holding on to my hand, then to let go and point her toe. Then Helen stands on my knee with out holding on to my hands and points her toe. Then I hold her up with my feet and she does a tummer sult off it. Then we get up and cursie and the to people at the end will close the doors quitly and the people go off stage in line QUITLY.

Conrad Krueger, an eight-year-old novelist who lives in Santa Monica, California, starts off his latest work in this fashion:

There was a big old idol in the temple, and when Jack entered he could smell the burning incest.

The fond parents of a nine-year-old Jackson Heights boy had signed him up for his first summer camp. As the day approached for his departure, they found themselves grieving over the impending separation. The mother finally went out and bought a nice leather notebook, with pencil attached. "I want you," she instructed her son, "to keep a diary, to write down every single detail of what happens while you are at the camp." He said he'd do it.

When at last he returned home his parents seized the little book and prepared themselves for several hours of pleasurable reading. They found that the boy had covered the first six pages with scrawly writing, as follows:

[97]

Thursday June 30

I arrived about 12 oclock and ate lunch. My concerlers name was Walter. We got cabin number 22 passed swimming test. List of names of campers in my cabin

John Hunter
Louis and Charles Concklin
Bruce Dobertene
Ray Wakeman

Friday July 1

Went swimming. In the night made a big fire and sung songs. We had a treasure hunt in the day.

Saturday July 2

Went on a nature hike some boys brought in a dead copper hed snake we skinned it. Then heard stories by Stan Le Von a jungel explorer he told us how he brought a dead man to life

Sunday July 3

Went to church. In the night Stan Le Von told stories and showed us a five foot snake.

Monday July 4

I got a letter from dad with a dollar bill in it we celabrated Indpendence day by reacting the Battle of Lexington.

Tuesday July 5

It was a very hot day.

Wednesday July 6

Got sunburn.

Thursday July 7

Got more sunburn.

Friday July 8

Are going to have a marshmellow roast. It was post-pond.

Saturday July 9

We were going to have a scavengar hunt. But it rained.

Sunday July 10

Routene.

Monday July 11

We had watermelon and Louis vomited.

Sunday July 17

It ended there — no entry under Sunday July 17, and no entry thereafter. An apt title for the whole thing might be: *The Petering Out of a Boy's Camp Diary*.

The Narramissic River is in Maine. It was the Narramissic, says E. B. White, that once received as fine a lyrical tribute as was ever paid to a river —

a line in a poem by a schoolboy, who wrote of it:

It flows through Orland every day.

There is an interesting form of creative literature practiced by very young children when they are alone, or think they are alone. It might be called "vocal writing." A fine example of it comes from Nancy D. Johnson, a Pennsylvania mother. When her younger daughter was just barely four, she began to make up lyrics while she was swinging. One warm day her mother quietly opened a window and copied the words sung out by the child as she swung to and fro. This is the way it went:

> They go somewhere
> When they go somewhere
> They did it
> When they did it
> They really did
> And I told them
> Not to go and do it
> They really did
> And when he goed home
> He ate it
> They just ate it
> When they wanted to
> They did eat the grass seed
> Little birdies ate it

When they did eat it
They did eat it
When they wanted to eat it
They did eat it
They did they did they did.

When I first got the above lyrics from Mrs. Johnson, I showed them to a literary friend of mine. He studied them briefly, then his face lighted up and he exclaimed, "My God, this is important! This child has finally given us the key to the writings of Gertrude Stein. It's as clear as daylight. Gertrude Stein had the mentality of a four-year-old!"

In her younger days, when she was around nine, Cassy Espy was a prolific writer of vigorous prose. Today she has little time for extracurricular composition because she is studying the harp and that keeps her pretty well occupied. Cassy's last writing of record, found nailed to a tree on the Espy property, was this:

to Who it May Concern
Do not fool around or ride my bike.
Cassy Espy

In more literary times Cassy turned out the following short story:

A NEW COMER

Patty was so exsited that she just Coudent ceep her mouth shaut.

Mommy Mommy she cried daddy says hes going to get a pony. Well this was going to far. patty you bring your father hear at once. Pritty soon they were there. Sam where do you get this pony stuf from. Now June I have plenty money. Yes but not so much that you can buy a PONY.

It was Sunday afternoon. the Stables were going to have a new comer. that was at lest what little Patty Gand thought. She was a blew eyd girl. She had red hair. her age was 7. ever sens she was 3 years old she had wanted a pony. But Mirs. Gand told her that it was two Much Money. Now Mister Gand thought that he had pretty much money.

So he thought that a little Black pony would be the new comer.

Almost as good as Faulkner, isn't it? Cassy has three sisters and since they are older they sometimes make life a little difficult for her. Two of them have boy names: Freddy and Joey. Here is a note Cassy composed:

Dear Freddy

I did not mean to get you in trouble but it seems you three older girls never include me in anything. and just because you are older than me you boss me around and say if I look at you stop looking at me.

[102   ]

I have a shoe untied so you say in Front of everybody stop looking like a slob.

Cassy

When my son was eight, he was gripped by the full fury of the souvenir bug. One summer he spent his vacation on his grandfather's farm in the middle of Missouri. When he returned home, he was loaded down with souvenirs. He had a basket full of rocks — just plain rocks. And he had a scrapbook into which he had glued certain gluable items, which were labeled:

> Lespideza from feild. Dont tuch.
> Clover from Clover feild. Dont tuch.
> Grass from front yard. Dont tuch.
> Grass from back yard. Dont tuch.
> Part of Hawker Hurricane. Dont tuch.

Nobody tuched although I spent a long time looking at one object, wondering how on earth he acquired part of a Hawker Hurricane on a remote Missouri farm.

Charles Morton of the *Atlantic Monthly* tells about a New England prep school boy who was writing home to explain his grades. He had flunked French, got a D in English and a C in mathematics, but he had done exceptionally well in navigation. His comment:

I am glad about that because navigation is something that I can use all my life.

Jonathan Cerf was quite negligent about writing to his Uncle Herbert and thanking him for his Christmas gift. When Jonathan finally got around to it he wrote:

Dear Uncle Herbert
I'm sorry I didn't thank you for my present and it would serve me right if you forgot about my birthday next Thursday.
Love, Jonathan.

A young woman who lives in Connecticut and who is the mother of two children has let me copy a letter she wrote about fifteen years ago. She was then twelve and had been sent to a boarding school for young girls. Her letter needs no explanatory notes, and reads:

Dearest dearest Mom & Dad,
Yes I still love Frankie. If it was not for him to sestain me I don't know what I would do I'm so home sick and I don't have one single friend. All the girls

like him to there is a girl here who is in love with that CREATURE Orsen Wells. Nobody speaks to her.

I got the higest mark in my Eng. comp. I got B— it doesn't seem good but all the other girls got C— & D except Susie & I & we got B—. I wish I was back in Ridgewood where they give grades that make sens.

Please please Please send me some fruit or cookies or candy ect. I like to eat a little while I study I can consintrate with food. *This is ergint.*

My brown shorts are to little I have to butten it at the second butten and I need some jodphers blue ones.

The important thing is we had pledging and just in case you don't know what pledging is I'll tell you. There are 2 soroties "Sigma Phy" and "A.T.G." I am being pledged into Sigma Phy. We were pulled out of bed at 6:00 and told to report to the polo field (thats where we ride) in 5 min. dressed in our Gymn shorts. Then we had to DUCK WALK all around the Polo field. Then climb walls, climb poles ect. Then we had to cut the grass on the polo field blade by blade and eat it. We have to wash our faces in the mud ect. Oh its awful. I have to work for my superior sister. Do anything she says.

The worst was Hell night which was last night and here's what they did. We ate (plain) garlick a big piece — Then a huge onion. Peanut Butter mixed with epsin salts. — Bread with Mineral Oil on the bread Perfume poured on our heads. Maccaronie (we thought it was worms) Then we walked blind folded (we were blind folded all the time) through a foot deep of mud & then had mud fight. I was so sick and we all smell of garlick it was so hard. You couldn't say ONE word or you got a protest and you were only aloud 3 protests but I didn't get any protests so I hope I will be excepted into the Sigma Phy. I don't have a single friend here which is the only thing that's wrong with it except that I am so home sick. But don't worry because it is all great fun and a wonderful experence and I think I will live through it.

x x x x x x x x x x x x x

Pam

Dr. George W. Crane has written of the Western motor tour taken by the Earl Edmondson family of Columbus, Ohio. The trip was planned largely for its educational value to the Edmondson children. Before they reached the Grand Canyon, Mr. Edmondson delivered a long and impressive build-up lecture. He spoke of the thousands of years it had taken to create the canyon and he told how people from Europe make the long trip just to have a look at this great scenic wonder.

Finally the Edmondsons stood on the brim of the canyon, regarding it with "awe and wonder" and taking photographs. Mr. Edmondson was aware of the fact that one of his young sons was keeping a diary of the trip. That night he managed to get hold of the diary; he wanted to see what the boy's reactions had been — if the build-up lecture had made a proper impression. He found, on the page devoted to the Grand Canyon, this single line:

Today I spit a mile.

The Edmondson story recalls another which I'm not able to give you. The one inviolable rule governing this collection forbids the use of "bright sayings of the children." I am prevented by that rule from repeating the Considine story. It goes as follows:

Bob Considine took one of his young sons, eight-year-old Dennis, on a trip to Washington, D. C., and spent an entire day showing him the historic wonders of the nation's capital. Mr. Considine had some trouble keeping his boy's attention, for he was like all other boys: constantly hungry and constantly thinking about something to eat. Mr. Considine made his lectures as graphic and as colorful as possible and it seemed to him that he was having pretty fair success, although Dennis spoke occasionally of being hungry. After a long tour of Washington proper they got in their car and started for Mount Vernon. On the way Mr. Considine spoke long and feelingly of George Washington. This was to be the high spot, the climax, of the tour. The boy appeared to be absorbing every word of it and finally they arrived at a place where they were to leave their car. They had to walk up a long slope before they could see the Mount Vernon mansion, and as they walked Mr. Considine continued his panegyric, getting the boy firmly in the mood for things to come. Suddenly they reached the crest of the hill and there before them stood George Washington's home. The boy's eyes widened and from his lips came the cry:

Oh, boy! A Howard Johnson!

It is too bad that the rules forbid my including stories like that in this book. Otherwise I'd be able to relate the tale told by Alexander Woollcott in his book *Long, Long Ago*. It is concerned with a little girl named Anna Lou, the daughter of a wealthy and socially prominent family in New Orleans. Even when she was five, Anna Lou's family had great plans for her, dreaming of the time when she'd take her place in genteel society. Whenever her mamma gave an elaborate dinner, Anna Lou was permitted, on her way to bed, to stop for a few moments and look at the great table with all its fine china and silver and napery. Then one evening, for the reason that Anna Lou had been naughty, this privilege was canceled and she was sent straightway to bed. At last the fashionable guests were assembled at the table and the dinner party was under way. Suddenly a big door opened slowly and through it appeared a small blond head and a clear soprano voice was heard, saying:

Ev'body in this room, 'ceptin me, is bitches.

Walter Russell Bowie, noted clergyman and author, once got a letter from a small boy who closed with:

I send you all my love and I hope you live all your life.

An unguarded typewriter in the home usually tempts the kiddies into trying their hands at authorship. Elmer Roessner, the New York newspaperman, had such a machine in his home when his two sons, Eugene and Donald, were young. Mr. Roessner sometimes found curious manuscripts left in the typewriter, but usually the best prizes were discovered by smoothing sheets that had been balled and thrown in a corner. When children start writing fiction, more often than not they abandon their work just as the story begins to get interesting. Mr. Roessner preserved two scripts typed out by his sons. The first follows:

CAPT. LIGHTFOOT

On a fogy night the ship Sun, set sail from Londen for wealth & fame. Capt. Lightfoot a tall sea faring man was at the wheel. His face was a brown and nicely shaped. His eyes whene pleased were a soft blue, but whene his temper was aroused they were like two percing sticks of dynamite. He sailed due south. When west of Spain a terific storm blew up. DOWN WITH THE

It ended right there. Apparently the dag-gone typewriter had gone completely and unchangeably caps, and the author abandoned his work in fear that he had broken the machine. At least that is the

father's theory. A week or so later another manuscript was discovered, as follows:

THE RANGER OF BLUE VALLY

He was all by himself in the vally exsept for his alla-
skin husky. His husky could tear a wolf apart and then
eat five poundes of meat. His masters name was Bill
(red) Roberts, beter known as Red Trouble. He had
spent ten years as a ranger, he is now head ranger of the
teritory within fifty miles of Blue Vally.

That's all. Not much plot.

The following two items are of questionable au-
thenticity, but they have become classics in our
field, so they must be included.

The first is a note written by a little girl to her
grandmother, or aunt (I've even heard it attributed
to Queen Victoria), which goes:

Thank you for your nice present. I always wanted a
pin cushion, although not very much.

The second illustrates how children, in their writing, are never hamstrung by tradition. The wisdom
of the ages impresses them not at all. They strike
out boldly for themselves, usually with a fine natu-
ralistic instinct. This little girl spent many weeks

cross-stitching a sampler for her favorite aunt, a maiden lady. When it was finally completed it bore the motto:

> Let me live in a house
> By the side of the road
> And be friendly with men.

How many times have you written a "thank you" note that was dishonest and insincere? Rules of etiquette insist that we dissemble in such notes and pretend something that often isn't true. Children, however, know little about the rules of etiquette, and care less. Usually they write their "thank you" notes under the supervision of their parents and the wording is the wording of the parents, not the children. Left to themselves, the little ones are inclined to give the adult world a lesson in sincerity. Mrs. Leon P. Gaucher of Beacon, N. Y., has had many "thank you" notes from children, but over the years she has only preserved one. If it were in her power, she says, she would knight the boy who wrote it. Here it is:

Dear Mrs. Gaucher:
   It is too bad you sent me that red truck for Xmas. I alreddy got one gist like it.

> Love,
> Bobby.

Nunnally Johnson, the brilliant Hollywood writer-director-producer, is blessed (or afflicted) with daughters who write. One of the girls, Marjorie, once turned out a long manuscript titled *The Autobiography of a Problem Child*. It was her intention

to submit it to the movies, but her father got hold of it first. "My hair turned plaid when I read it," Mr. Johnson said. He quickly closed a deal with Marjorie, purchasing all rights to the story, then buried it in quicklime.

Another Johnson daughter, Christie, fell in love

at the age of five and addressed the following poem to the boy of her dreams:

Hide the truth of our love from everybody but me,
Because I'm in love with you as who can see.

Nora Johnson's flair for writing was journalistic. When she was ten she produced her own newspaper, called *Mairsy-Doats*. The name itself seems to me to be an inspiration and I recommend it to Roy and Jack Howard. I'd be much more inclined to buy a newspaper called the Cleveland *Mairsy-Doats* than one bearing the commonplace title Cleveland *Press*.

Nora's *Mairsy-Doats* was a newspaper dedicated to eternal resistance to tyranny — the tyranny of parents. The editorials slashed at these dictators and their stupid ideas, which they were forever trying to palm off on their betters, i. e., their children. Two of Nora's fighting editorials follow:

CLEANLINESS IS *NOT* NEXT TO GODLINESS!

We have discovered that in the soap factory they throw the soap by bushels into dirty old tubs, they don't care what happens to it, and most of the soap you get has been left standing at least two weeks. They call it anything they can think of and the labels are mixed. Soap is impure to the body and creates a rash on the limbs.

CANDY

One of the most nutritious foodstuffs is that delicious object, manufactured all over the world, namely, candy. There are lots of kinds of candy, old-fashioned sugarplums, stick candy, molasses, fudge and candy drops. The two principal classes of candy are hard candy and soft candy and they're both good. DID YOU KNOW THAT candy and sodas and sundaes and ice cream of all kinds have more vitamins and calories than any food in the world? That fudge should be made every day to sustain life?

When the late Alexander Woollcott was ten, he went to a children's party in suburban Philadelphia. At one point the guests were asked to write down their fondest ambitions. Little Alec was almost prophetical in his response. He wrote:

I would rather be a Fabbulous Monster.

Among the more widely known compositions produced during the television age is that of a schoolboy who was told to write a report on the church service he attended. He wrote:

I liked the music okay but the commercial was too long.

Arthur Godfrey's son Mike entered a radio contest when he was eight years old. It was required that contestants write, in twenty-five words or less, the reason why they favored a certain program. Mike's entry:

I like the Jack Smith show because as soon as it is over the Lone Ranger comes on.

When Lyn Laird arrived at the age of seven her parents decided it was time she was told about poetry. In describing the art to her, they gave emphasis to the importance of rhyme, reciting several simple examples. Then they gave her pencil and paper and asked her to try her hand at making a rhyme. She stewed and ruminated for a long while, and then wrote:

The horns were loose
On the moose

Mrs. Henry D. Haas of Granville, Ohio, has sent me a twelve-page book that was written, illustrated and stapled by her daughter Donna at the age of seven. The crayon illustrations take up much more space than the text, which follows:

THE WUNDERFUL WATER
AND MY WISH

One warm summer day the Wunderful Water was walking in the woods when he mant a rubbit. then the wunderful water said "what is your wish today my friend Mrs. ribbit? Mrs. rabbit said "I wist to have twenty five Babies in one day and six fathers in a week.

Then the wunderful water said "That will be find he said but you must be married first to a man rubbit. what? she said "you must be merried first. me be meriet huh she said." and what dus that mein.

It meins that you can not have twenty five babies in a day. But you can have them latter.

So Mrs. rubbit got merried and lived
happle ever after
With thear 13 girls and 12 boys.

Leane Zugsmith, novelist and short-story writer, grew up in Atlantic City and as a small girl spent a lot of time experimenting with the novel form. One of her earliest efforts for some reason got only this far:

THE FLOWER MAID

There was once a beautiful lady, Margery, who had a husband and he belonged to the Civil War and his name was George Washington and

Little Leane also tried her hand at a novel called *The Jealous Woman*. The name of this jealous woman was Stella and she had a terrible quarrel with her husband, after which:

One day Stella went to another town called Bachelorsville where thousands and thousands of Bachelors lived; all you could see was Bachelors. Stella's husband had once been a Bachelor and she saw his Monument here (in that time it was much differenter than now) and Stella took a heavy iron broom and knocked her husband's Monument down. She stamped on it even, she was so glad no one could make her wear a cross face any more.

When he was ten Theodore Roosevelt was taken on a trip to Europe. He kept a diary in which there were frequent references to the poor state of his own health. He wrote, for example, of his recovery from "an attack of asmer" and of a dream:

I had a dream that the devil was carrying me away and have collerer morbus, a sickness that is not at all dangerous.

According to *Newsweek*, a schoolboy wrote to the Library of Congress:

Can you give me the name of a good book on aeronautics and one on sane sex life? I am more interested in aeronautics.

I can't remember where I got hold of it, but for some years I've had tucked away in my files an item labeled "The very first writing of James Thurber." It is nothing more than the title of a poem, minus the poem itself. Here it is:

> My Aunt Mrs. John T. Savage's Garden
> at 185 South Fifth Street, Columbus,
> Ohio.

I think you'll agree that there's a lovely lyrical quality to that title. I became so familiar with it that I learned it by heart and sometimes at parties I'd even recite it. It was always my intention to get in touch with Mr. Thurber and ask him for the poem that went under the title. Finally I got around to it. Mr. Thurber informed me that the title was actually:

My Auntie Margery Albright's Garden,
185 South 5th Street, Columbus, Ohio.

What a crushing blow! I read it over in his version, again and again, and the more I read it the less
I liked it. I had it firmly fixed in my mind that the
title was "My Aunt Mrs. John T. Savage's Garden
at 185 South Fifth Street, Columbus, Ohio." Who
did this Thurber think he was, to come along and
change it to "My Auntie Margery Albright's Garden, 185 South 5th Street, Columbus, Ohio," and
remove all the compelling beauty from it? To me it
was the same as if Henry Wadsworth Longfellow
sent word that the way he really wrote it was:

> Listen my children, don't bare your claws,
> While I tell of the ride of William Dawes.

In time I may come to accept Auntie Margery
Albright as belonging to the property at 185 South
5th Street, Columbus, Ohio. There is no doubt that
she *did* belong to it, and if there ever was a Mrs.
John T. Savage, she didn't have a garden at 185
South 5th Street, Columbus, Ohio. Mr. Thurber
has written a wonderful sketch of Mrs. Margery Albright in *The Thurber Album* and has even included a photograph of her, sitting in her famous
garden and holding a potted azalea.

Mr. Thurber was unable to supply the verses that went with the title. He seems to be a man who remembers titles more than text; his first prose writing, produced when he was about ten, bore the title "Horse Sandusky the Intrepid Scout." The story itself apparently has been lost forever. And Mr. Thurber, thinking back to the childhood compositions of his daughter, can recall only the way they started out. One of her early efforts, written when she was nine, began:

Linda Whitney was the youngest F. B. I. agent. She was eighteen.

"I think," says Mr. Thurber, "that children are better at writing letters than anybody, all the way back to Madame de what's-her-name. I once sent my daughter a doll from Rome which took me a hell of a time to get bought and through the customs. She was seven and she acknowledged the gift as follows:

Dear Daddy,
        Thanks for the doll I can skate

"It seems to me," Mr. Thurber observes, "that American businessmen, and American writers, too, could learn something from all this, such as how to get your work done faster and live longer."

With a nod, then, to Mr. Thurber, I offer herewith a letter in which an eight-year-old Los Angeles girl manages to pack a lot of news into a few words:

Dear Uncle Tony

How are you feeling. Just last week a car ran into the front of a house in the living room. He didn't inger or kill anyone. Then of all things he got out of his car and sat down at the kitchen table and the lady said thank God you didn't kill anyone and the man said I don't believe in God. So the sherif came and took him away. Grandma has had double pnewmonia. Well good by for a while I will write you soon.

love
Cheryl

Last February Police Chief J. C. Macdonald of Memphis found himself in possession of more than nine hundred essays written by boys from seven to twelve years old. Each boy was seeking the job of Junior Police Chief during Crime Prevention Week in Memphis and was required to write out his ideas on law enforcement.

Lydel Sims of the *Commercial Appeal* went

through the essays and reported on some of them as follows:

"Anyone hanging around stores after they have closed should be questioned and took home," one boy wrote, adding, "All women should stay in after dark and all dogs should be tied."

A candidate named Graham explained that the best way to get eye witnouses to creams is to question all suspicious persons. He added, however, that he would never shrech a house without a shrech wort.

An eight-year-old's platform for chiefhood included this: "Listen for shouts. Be ready for anything. Not make any deals with mysterious looking people."

A boy named Kenneth said he would fine people "that even had an intoxicaten liquid on them," but another named Tommy recommended "a limit of two jiggers of whiskey a day if you drank whiskey."

A nine-year-old promised desperately that he'd "woke hard to invent Crime," while another proposed not shooting anybody until you gave him time to draw his gun.

John said every policeman should know Marse Code. Rodger offered to install burglar alarms that would drop something on burglars' heads and knock them out. Jerry suggested more playgrounds and jims.

A ten-year-old candidate wrote: "I would try to prevent crime by trying to improve the ways of frustration." One way of improving frustration, he explained, just in case he hadn't made himself clear, would be to point the coat hangers in different directions when you hang up a lot of mink coats.

Two seventh-grade girls collaborated on the following scientific paper:

EXPERIMENT

First we took a Jar and filled it with vinegar. then we put chicken bones into the vinegar. we let the bones stay in the vinegar for several days.

we took the bones out of the vinegar and they appeared to be rubber like and spongey.

the calcium and Phos Phorus had been destroyed by the Conclusion. Calcium and Phos Phorus are needed for strong bones.

Just as so many other scientists arrive at faulty conclusions, those two girls fell into error. They should have said that calcium and Phos Phorus are needed for strong bones provided you are a chicken.

Mrs. W. R. Pope of Oklahoma City reports that there are two poems that have become classics in her family. Her cousin, when he was nine, produced the following:

> Alone, Alone, Alone
> In the dark.
> Not a creature was stirring,
> Not even a stork.

His sister's first bit of writing was a thank-you note to her grandmother which read:

> Thankey for the
> Hankey.

Once upon a time when I was prowling through the 1907 files of my home-town newspaper, I came upon a story about a boy named Tom Barker who, for pulling a girl's hair, had been ordered to stay after school and write a composition of fifty words. This is what he wrote:

Jessie was fond of kittens. She saw one in the road and called, "Here, pussy."

All parents of children who have teeth (the children, not the parents) will recognize a common household condition as set forth in Katinka Matson's thank-you note. Last Christmas we sent a supply of scratch pads and pencils to the four Matson children, and received the following note from Katinka:

Dear Nelle and Allen,

Thank you so much for the pencils and pads. I needed then so much because it seems the pencils around our house seem to be eaten up.

Love,
Tinka.

Earlier this year the Montebello Soroptimist Club sponsored a safety contest among school children. Matt Weinstock of the Los Angeles *Mirror-News* reports that a second-grader named Marilyn Mears turned in the following:

I was crossing Atlantic
When the light was not green.
If I had looked I would have seen.
I fell to the ground
People gathered around.
'Be calm' they said.
But it was too late,
I was already dead.

Mrs. Gordon Lewis remembers that when she was nine years old she sent her favorite aunt a home-made birthday card, bearing the following sentiment:

Now that you are thirty one
Your old days have begun.
Happy birthday!

An old, old theme is given a rather fresh look in this bit by a child in a Long Island school:

WHEN I GROW UP

When I grow up I want to cach like Yogi Bear.

The following seasonal story was written by Robert Sims at the age of eleven. I don't know whether Robert was trying to be humorous, or just describing life as it is. His story:

A MOTHER'S DAY SURPRISE

It was Sat. and the Doolittle children were jabbering away. Oscar Doolittle said, "Tomorrow is Mother's Day and I think it would be nice if we bought her a present.

Herman Doolittle said, "Now, ain't that reel smart? That's the first nice thing you said since you was born."

Their sister, Maggie, said, "I think we should get her a hat."

So the trio went down town and went to eleven different stores, but none had what they wanted. After an hour's search, they got what they wanted, a hat.

When they got home they hid it in their room. When Sun. came they got the present and marcher into their mother's room! "Surprise! Surprise! Come on, get up you lazy bone — woman. We have a surprise for you."

(Several min. later) "Well, do you like it?" asked Oscar. "Yes! Yes! But what is it?"

"A hat," said Maggie. "Oh, yes, it's beautiful! Thank you very much," said their mother. "What a surprise this is!"

Miriam Young, author of *Mother Wore Tights*, inaugurated her literary career with a modern-day *Odyssey*, dashed off at the age of six:

> As we went to Philadelphia on the train,
> It began to pour and then to rain.

In a recent book, *The Grass Is Never Greener*, a young Canadian humorist named Robert Thomas Allen quotes a letter he received from his little niece in Sarnia. It goes:

Dear Uncle Bob: I fell in the river yesterday. I like being wet. Sally had four kittens. I saw a skunk. Joan won't let me play with her doll. I hope she dies. I hope you are well. Love . . .

Jim Street's daughter, Ann, is a handsome young lady today. When she was a little girl she spent a summer at a New England camp. One day four letters came to our house. Save for the salutations, the wording of the letters was exactly the same, as follows:

There is not much to do. I don't have any thing to do. I don't have much to say. I just wanted something to do. I am in rest hour.

Love, Ann.

Mrs. Robert E. Peppers of Herculaneum, Missouri, remembers the little poem she wrote when her favorite teacher was stricken ill and taken to a hospital. The poem, which was intercepted by her mother and never reached the sick teacher, went this way:

Dear Miss Randall:
Sorry you're sick
And lying in bed.
Hope you come back
Before you're dead.

Miss Sally Ofield is a qualified author at the age of seven. Her achievement was recently reported by Malcolm Epley in the *Press-Telegram* of Long Beach, California.

Sally's mother attended a class in creative writing at City College in Long Beach. One day she brought Sally to class, for Sally had written a story. It was read aloud and the students, in their comments, gave it their full approval. It follows:

LETITIA WANTS TO GET MARRIED

One morning Letitia sat in bed. She got on her pink dress and wanted to see Tom.

Letitia had blue eyes, black hair. "Tomorrow I'm going to get married to Tom. I love Tom, and he loves me."

It was time to put on her wedding dress. Tom put on his tuxedo. They were married.

"Oh, Tom, I love you!"

"And I love you, too."

Then Letitia kissed him. "I love you, Tom."

Letitia wanted to have a baby. She got one.

"Oh, Tom, come here."

"What is it?"

"My baby. It's here. Hurry, Tom!"

"Is it a boy or a girl?"

"I do not know."

THE END

Here's another one of those maddening short stories that seem to come to an abrupt and unsatisfying end, this one the work of a ten-year-old lass:

Once there was a little girl. She was in a horse show. She wanted to win something in the horse show. She was doing very well but she didn't hold her knees tight and keep her heels down. The next day the little girl named Jane ate. Then she said what can I do. think her mother said. I can not think she said. feed your horse Blue Bell. of yes said the little girl. She fed her horse and rid him

[130   ]

Mrs. Warren G. Holste of Fort Kobbe in the Canal Zone tells me of the time her daughter, Barby, decided to run away from home. The Holstes were making plans to attend a movie one evening and Barby, who was seven, wanted to go. She was told firmly that she could not go. So she flounced out of the room and went upstairs. A short time later Mrs. Holste went up and found Barby in her room, furiously packing a bag. On the bed were Barby's doll, Margie, and two sheets of paper.

As Mrs. Holste entered the room Barby picked up one of the sheets of paper and thrust it at her. Scrawled on it were the words:

I am running away forever and I am taking Margie with me.

Mrs. Holste could not restrain herself. She burst into laughter. Whereupon Barby grabbed the other sheet of paper and flung it toward her mother. It said:

Dont laugh. I really am.

A bit later Barby calmed down and changed her plans. "To this day," says her mother, "I don't know how she knew I would laugh."

A teacher told her pupils to "write a sentence with the word 'analysis' in it." One boy, who hadn't been paying attention when the word was defined, turned in the following:

I looked up the word 'analysis' in the dictionery.

Bennett Cerf tells about an exchange of notes between a boy and a girl in the third grade. The boy wrote:

Dear Judee: I luv you. Do you luv me? Jimmy.

The girl promptly answered:

Dear Jimmy: I do NOT love you. Love, Judy.

It may be that the children of Beverly Hills are more worldly and sophisticated than in other communities. Libbie Block has sent me a report on a seven-year-old boy in Beverly Hills, a boy who has been undergoing a series of medical tests. He was a conscientious patient and took it all quite seriously. One day his mother found a milk bottle on a table in his room, and propped against it was a printed sign which warned:

> There is pea in this bottle
> for the Dr. Be carful.

I think it was nice of that boy to leave the warning sign, but I also think it was unnecessary. Anybody who came along and failed to be carful . . . well, they'd deserve exactly what they got.

A young East Side matron sent the *New Yorker* an essay on herself, composed by her eight-year-old daughter. It read:

THINGS ABOUT MY WONDERFUL, WONDERFUL MOTHER

1. She's clean.
2. She's not selfish.

3. She's got a good sence of hummer.
4. She likes to read.
5. She sews with her left hand.
6. She's got a timper.

Laurette Howars has recorded the following essay in *As a Child Sees:*

SMELLS

Smells are things to know about. When people do good things, they smell sweet. When they do bad things, they do not smell sweet at all. Dogs know about this.

A little girl, writing in Sunday school, described the sufferings of Job in this manner:

Job had one trouble after another. First he lost his cattle then he lost his children then he had to go live in the desert with his wife.

When Don Gaucher was ten years old and attending summer camp, he wrote a letter home to his mother, never suspecting that his message has been a favorite of the jokesmiths for years. Don's letter:

Dear Mom:
If we do not write a letter home today we can not have any lunch —
Very Truly Yours
Don.

Mrs. John Seymour Orr of Detroit was looking up a word in the dictionary recently when she came upon a brief manuscript. It had been hidden away in the big book for fifteen years, the work of the Orrs' daughter, Mary, when she was eight. Here it is:

MY POPS ADVENTURES IN
THE FIRST WARLD WAR

He started out as twenty one years old. The first

place he went was Camps Custer in Battle Creek Michigan. That is where he got his rokey training. After he had much hard work he was transfered to Camps Lee Virginia Which is in Virginia near Petersbrug where he sucesfuly passed his first Examination and became a second Luetenant. Then he Went to France on the way across the ocean he saw a German sub. and also he was on watch in the crows nest of the ship. He had interresting experiencis and after came down with the flu. He did not die.

— Mary Orr, and in
colaberation with J. S. Orr.

Nancy Blanford of Scarsdale remembers a Mother's Day poem that should delight the eye of Philip Wylie. It was written by her sister Ginny when she was seven, and reads:

> You're as sweet as
>   sugar candy
> You're as sweet as
>   apple pie,
> You're no better than
>   any other mother,
> But, boy, how you try!

For mothers who might feel hurt by Ginny's sentiments, there is compensation in a poetic bit written by a child in Illinois:

THE WORKING WOMAN

The working woman goes about
   In and Out
And dusts the room
   All nice and clean
And then she strings the bean.

When my first small collection of children's writing appeared in *Good Housekeeping*, it caught the attention of Mrs. William H. Deily of Oreland, Pennsylvania. Mrs. Deily summoned her eight-year-old daughter Brenda and asked her to write a story for my collection. Brenda finished the job in fifteen minutes and her story follows:

MAN KILLER

Once upon a time there was an elafent and he was called man killer becuase he could kill iny man in the jungle.

One day a man said im not afrade of man killer. So he went into the jungle. About one hour later he saw man killer so he shot at him hopeing to hit him right betwen the eyes but he mist the hole elafent. And the elafent went after him. About 5 mintes later man killer killed him. And when all the other people heard about this they said that the man that was killed by man killer should have thout that when your going to do something that you know you can't do you shount do it.

A mother in upstate New York has copied down poems written by her two sons when they were around seven years old. Both of them are now over six feet tall and she says they will "have a fit" if they find out the poems have been shown to strangers. So, with no names, here are the poems:

ROBIN HOOD

there dwelt Sherwood forest
a very helpfull man
Whose name was Robin Hood
and joyfully ruled his band
He always helped the poor
and allways robbed the rich
dont you think thats better
than digging in a ditch

SUMMER

Summer is hot I am too
I think its hot dont you
The sun is hot as hot as the equater
Its getting so hot I'm beginning to hate her.

Now at the end of this book I'd like to offer my qualifications as its author. A biography, setting forth my attainments in life and letters, was put together about fifteen years ago. It was written, without my knowledge or consent, on both sides of the paper, partly in pencil and partly in ink. The author apparently composed it in the back of the house while I was turning out lesser prose up front. She wrote it and then hid it away and forgot about it, but such literary masterpieces have a way of turning up in time, and I present it in print, uncorrected, for the first time:

THE LOWEST MAN IN THE PUTTY KNIEF FACTORY

By N. J. Smith

Introduction

You will probably wonder about the Title of this story. It is to include the life thus far of my Father H. Allen Smith. He is an author and has to this day has written two best-seller novels. The names of them were Low Man on a Totum Pole and Life in a Putty Knief Factory. Therefore I have combined the two names and entitled it "The Lowest Man in the Putty Knief Factory."

Chapter One

H. Allen Smith was born in Maclainsbourg Ill. Dec. 19. He is a medium sized fellow with blue eyes brown hair, Although it is rapidly decreasing day after day, and is rather thin, but as his years pass I believe he will get broader. He is married to my mother who is a very bright lovely lady in her late thirties. She has Silver hair and a snazzey figure. Besides myself there is one more in the Smith family. It is my brother. He has brown hair and is quite cute, although Id never tell him that, he is one of these genuises in school & has very little comon since out side of school. He is one year older than I am and has about six years more since than I do.

My father has lived in the United St all of his 3? years and has never been abroad Although I beleive once he went on a hunting trip in Canada. When he was quite young he had to quite school in the 9th grade and go to work. He lied his way into the newspa-per business and soon after he went to Florida where he met my mother. They were married in 1927. Then my father took a job on the "Denver Post" and both my brother & I were born in Denver. But then the family dicided to move to N. Y. We came with no money but little enought to rent a house and keep us alive. We moved to a little town in the suberb of Queens named J. Heights. My father then managed to obtain a job with one of the newspapers I beleive it was the News. Then as he got use to N. Y. C. & the life of a newspaperman we moved to various apts in J. Hgts. Then out to the country. Then when I was about 7 we moved to Astoria and lived there for about 1 year. But then my father obtained a job with the "World Telegram" and got experiance as the weather reporter. Then we moved back to J. Hgts and lived in that house for about 5½ years. Then daddy decided to quit the Telegram and write for mag. & books ect. He wrote 2 unsucesful books then finally he wrote "Low Man on a totum Pole" in 1941 and it became a best seller. We then moved to the "Tower Apts" in J Hgts having three bathrooms and a fire place where he wrote "L. in a P. K. Factory."

That seems to be the conclusion of it. Until I saw the manuscript I hadn't realized just how dreary my life had been. I tried to convince myself that she really hadn't finished the biography — that she saved

the livelier bits for later on and then never got around to writing them. She neglected to mention that I once swam the Ohio River, that I was personally acquainted with the inventor of the Meyer Reversible Jiffy Bow Tie, that I can read a page of print upside down almost as fast as I can read it rightside up, and that as a child I suffered a severe head injury. She didn't cut off the narrative for lack of paper because there was room for more prose on the final page. Instead of examining into the beautiful nature and personality of her subject, however, she had written in this blank space:

$$(3 \text{ a x b}) - 2 \text{ x } (2 \text{ A x B})$$
$$\text{x} \quad (2 \text{ X}$$

Those symbols may look mysterious, but to me they have meaning. They stand for an awful lot of foolishness that came after "L. in a P. K. Factory." And it hasn't ended yet.